NOTER DAMUS

Books by Joyce James

CHRONICLES

The Judas Compound (1994)

POETRY

Selected Poems 1960-1980 (1984)

CHAPBOOKS

The Craft of Inner Space (1970)

ESSAYS

Shouted From The Housetops (1964)

Joyce James

NOTER DAMUS

PAST AND FUTURE ANNALS OF THE GRAIL

Ladan Reserve Press

Ladan Reserve Press
P.O. Box 881239
Steamboat Plaza
CO 80488-1239 USA

ISBN
Softcover 0-9629287-6-3
Hardcover 0-9629287-4-7

Printed and bound in the United States of America

Library of Congress Cataloging-in-Publication Data

James, Joyce.
Noter Damus : past and future annals of the grail / Joyce James.
p. cm.
Abridged version of: An unorthodox world history according to the goddess, Our Lady Mother.
ISBN 0-9629287-6-3 (pbk. : alk. paper) -- ISBN 0-9629287-4-7 (alk. paper)
1. Goddess religion--Poetry. I. James, Joyce. Unorthodox world history according to the goddess, Our Lady Mother. II. Title.
PS3560.A385 N+

2002031339

The Dedication

In The Beginning
Maide Dove Ma-Manna
The Sound Was Her Word,
Notated Her Utterance Maide
World D.N.A...

GODDESS
DI.AN.A

The Contents

Chap-Books In Brief

BOOK ONE

GENESIS

Life Intelligence, known to Herself alone...
Existence All-Being, She is but One...
Who spins the systems teeming-moons,
Welds the minerals, solar suns,
Atomi that loose-appointed
Chord Her Purpose: Sonne-Clé.

Think on it! The vastness is Her Mind!
Concept so encompassing,
Does only yawn,
Simplistic id-iota idly springs our own.
No question is there life on Mars:
Mars itself is Life:
And we who equally share that life... in part are also Mars.

Sentient is all space which pulses galaxies Her bloodstream,
Orbits precious jewels, the planets,
Conscious wanderers so august:
Yet amount attributes these not more than atoms
Studding Minne-Scule The Form Divine Her Body.

Her Star alighted over Arcady. Interlocked.
(Wobbled still the molten skew rang mostly brittle iron.)

Was to know the lack of nothing, Her Great Plan,
School-École She Maide Complete,
Her creatured World and Man,
Wherein should parse the Gramary composing him...
Imbue capacities of mutation that would evolve,
Provide the further evolution....
Not all is shown him...
Bifurcate mentate tendrilled,
Prosthesis the pattern Her own,
Innate was meant to formulate,
To fractalate geometries
Mapping curling life organic,
Budded turbulate diversity;
To arc in involuted coiling piling infinite;
Reiterate perpetuity (irrelevant how abstract),
Issue spirogram projections
Rooted in the matrix source.

She breathed Her Breath on living rock,
Crumbling innermost cells to quicken them vaporous;
Separated particles, and molecular parsed the waters
Rained on granular gleaming facet,
Exposing of all, first solar light
That formed and bred the soul-blocks
Maide original KaBonne Life:
Responded Breath of Brooding Spirit -
New Element A-Rose -
To generate each armature and scaffolding of Form,
Proclaiming every spectrum of Creation Her Delight:
Helices sang its chording,
Her Æearth Prodigious,

Drawn and drawing spirograph of farthest stars -
First burgeoning complexities appear as verging chaos:
Yet emerges from proliferation near infinite tonality,
New Choirs and Orders Maide Our Lady Dia Né:

DIANA

BOOK TWO

LADAN

Fire was in him.
Buried deep as writhed the central earth
And it flickered the depths of his eye
Probing fitful through far distance,
Lit segment spokes of iris that divided,
Viewed internal life-fire as if through beams not seen connected,
Selecting here and yonder unknowable extrusions,
Contours of the smoldering shell;
Making stars of them which were reflection of his inner burnings.

His name was L'Adan.
Creature bore us pain and suffering. Fathered sorrow.

The fire was deep within him and separate from night-waters
Surging dispatch of their concourse,
Goutings moved the channeled frame,
Parsed together float and jetsam, element and airy matter,

Light was also in him. It was good.
Not good, darkness.
Uneasy to and fro its tides, consuming weight and the denser air.
No. He must not ponder hell or burning.

Thus was he.
Of elements distant:
Earth and water, air and fire,
Bondings purposed indissoluble,
Smilings of eden and airiest hell.
Demarcations separate mapped deep waters' rising knowledge of all
He would become:

The good. Then shadow fallen to evil
Full four the seasons,
Would lathe century cyclings...
Rotation his turnings, short night and its day;
Resonance keyed on wandered stars that flickered light above him.

He knew that the sky-fire would likely come back,
Arising low slanting the First Other Side -
Where reversal was found - all things their Shadow.

Had always thus far, Solar Deus, made presence substantial again,
Shone golden appointment His new risen dawn
On the Other Side of Dark.

BOOK THREE

NOTER DAMUS

Dispatched once more the Ash-Ash life,
Returns again to cruxe as Infant Maide new L'Ankh-Aster-Starte
Arriving Isis Black Poulaye belayed fowl scheme en-sor-celling
Led ash-worth's scaffold five-bard gait -
Gate five-barred was laine black pool re-dubbed abuse Ab-Houston -
There lain as prey of fell phy-sickans - men smashed lives and hearts -
Grucifying broken jambes on pegma borne dream-circled freight
Portended death - noose hung hungry in the square,
Where reigned La Reine's ChaTod'Arques San-Guinarchy...
Guinocol and yoniversity nurtured Sanguine Blood its women.

Gazing through glazed wind-ows which seemed never to reveal,
A student schooled the House of Caer and Myriad Paning, she would learn
Of Wind soared Royal Height where oracular soars the Poet his sor-cery;
Of wind, sore lost the heart-breath was her child-born;
Of wind, sore lost the windpipe, strictured near closing her own.

Wind spirular the lessonings our history,
As we confront again what came before.
Was thought would familiar usage harden us,
Perhaps not to flinch at the end. No.
Unless is found such chance event the end
Contingent with our own.

Noter Damus: Joyce Hilary James.

(JHJ: courtesy a-ward of Guardians of The Poor Law.)

J'aimes I love: L'Oeuf Lo-vie Le Vi.
Povra pauper Pura-belle Victimidry Rode trussed,
Blackpudlin dublinguin dovetailed Joyce of Triste tris-tanus,
To James adds shames for the constant contympun.
Yet do legacies four descend from The Dove.
Enraptured by Her revelations, Magistic Columbnar Sound,
Ever came Joyous Her love.

(Eh! Them were't times we lived through. Them were't times all right!
But best of all we survive 'em, try any way to change 'em...
Even getting born again to make the terra firma more than humer.
Ex. Hume. ill. I. ate! Again I am here and eaten alive....
Roasted the fat of the land of the dead.
Humeroast was her father, so the mother said!)

Does Bean-vegetarian, Leg-humarian sound like nonsense?
The family putatively mine, alongside James,
Referred to itself as Hume. Jambes Leg-Humes. Legumes distinctive.
Leg again you see. Legatease? Double Joyce and Double James?

Twice does love, then 'J'aimes' again, the Legs Trois J'aimbes!
Portend those 'I's' of triple bleeding, the eyes of bloodiest dream.

By official dispensation become henceforth, ' Joyce James '.
A name misleading bore no approximation of a joyous life fulfilled,
But would my legs, les jambes, afford great pleasure and delight
(Unforeseen lain thieving day such joys were rendered forfeit:
But pulverized The Jambe-Bone - was needed ever joyous,
Mes jambes - my legs -
Seeming signal J'aimes meant life not wholly bad...
Leg-acy of love came A-**leg**-ria, a joyousness of dancing limbs).

Next appendaged A-leg-ria:
Twice is Joyous! The husband Mr.James:
Ergo! Joyce James Doubled Dove-lin! Dub the Dove-line,
Arrives the Coney-life of troublesome haire, eyelascelus rabbit,
Heir (too ironic!) to joy - its supposed Leg-a-Tiy.
Mix cilia heir the Hilary as did Dub-liner, James Joyce -
Then are accessed names arcane: Joy'cilia hillary and Larry Hill-ary,
High-Larynx Chanter-Clair the dawn Poulaye, Haute Lauryate Hi-Lares,
Poet Tutelary to the household spirited thence reluctant...
LaPis-ex-ilias: La Pis, the way of the exile and X-unknown:

Exile excilius: destitute and paupered. One of Slender Means.
(Not shared with her rich Coney life and golden hoard came Goshen.)

Transfixed in the future not revealed, grieves piteous crouch La Pietà -
Petrifies the broken heart, transforms to Stone the vessel acid etched -
Pavéed LaPis! (The Way) then beaten worse, La-Pis The New Exilias:
Grail Maide Stone.. and straitened her means, Hail Airy Grail Gracilus,
A Grace bloom Columbine Aquilegia Gracilus, Granna O'Malley's nightcap.

No dolor of the mortal heart consoled nor repaired a femme-oral sharded.
No more might bear pythonic weight, the Femme Bonne.

La Derelitta now! Beggared Sister Poverty, The Merry Maide,
Who sounded and created genetic braidings helical
That reticulate instruction,
Maintain the infra-bio-worlds comprise the living DNA.
Stollen now her grimoires white - as were Maman's.

Joyous was Diana!
Yet agelong pain unfurls Her-Story, insoluble yoked with his,
Antagonist eternal, The Apollo is Her twin:
Who advocates agenda eliminates the female

That men themselves may bear new life;
Effect redundancy of Woman: accomplish abolition
Of Lilium Her Majesty A-Rose The Venus Aphro-Dit!

From templates magic-keyed and coding thence the female womb,
Were pirated the genes, spliced and thence recombinant,
Produced the mascule altered next:
Devil-brew that breathed as rogue released from hell,
Mal-Magda-Androgue-Gynn:
Monsieur La Freak performing dual, was also Le Madame!
With entitlement exquisite: **Le Magdalen! Ventura.**

Thing suckles a sort of human infant!
Shuffling bearded hangdog herme a pharaditic,
Grown malignancy maternal! Unnerves this Ma-scule Le Mammaria
Maide declining conjugations that are nowhere lawful -
Maide Demasia Dammed.
(Performs beyond fem-surrogate,
The Abo-minne from bio-gennet manipulated change.)
But nothing less than global is envisioned for its advent:
Ap-Hominidae Venturo spreads new virulence Ventura.
Natura Demente! Anatomy ready!

What does it serve Abomin-anomaly?
How understood the twisting of life,
Male-diction mal-featus seems genus transformed?
Maide vassal enslaved to Apollo! Conscripted toiler
Apocalyptic cosmic ignocript! Perverted Apolloco-lip-sic
To orchestrate and resonate his-peiny hiss,
The Heralding of humankind's annihilation.

Domestic life is meant to vanish: by militant mascule be subsumed.
Annihilated those species breeding non-carnivorous -
And will former human female-kind be banished -
Vanquished or replaced each one
By project-warlock spawns subhuman army
Obedient in nothing beyond pursuit of single task:
Its commerce and labor obtaining the gold.

Profaned! The Primal Seal.

Maide star-stud Hers! to prop satanic rib the bio-gallo gallows-tree!

Granted life sacred our great La Vi, sanctioned Humanity's inception.
Iniquity! that appointed Cells Divine within faculty so degraded.

Now fends its death! The Bearer of Life:
Musters every device saves Woman's demise.

For treasure that is Earth, to tempt him ever further,
Implacable antagonad determined on the prize his Sister's world,
Benevolence breathes measured Matro-Nomic over fragrance that is eden.

An ambition that is boundless reaches to dominion -
With humanity eternally suborned in servitude inimical.
Implanted within it lies conscience false
So basely felt as love of gold,
And fashioned thence to dream:
Precisely that same dreaming engineers,
Imposes slavery brute-bondage
Labors the length of mortal lives...
Orbus robota scrabbled after Ophir gold...

Providing him, maintaining him in stollen lusts unholy,
The gilded viper Apellon!
Sod-popper maculosus glides serpent-smooth the massacurst.

(Should creep both word and penance Gaelic! His-Pein!

Her-pein indeed! Never word of Hers!
Never crawler, or snake-like She!
Except plume sped curled the serpentine wake
Of Her ship dove galactic Her skies.)

No moon the Cow-Horned Goddess, horns mean fertile Her Crescent.

Bitter gall the blood feud determines domination of Her Earth!
And gravity compounding, must She fund and underwrite atrocity
By gouging from Earth Her own gold!

* * *

Roams sacred no longer Our Sky-Goddess-Vox...
Moonrover Golden The Heifer.
By venting of vengeance Iodic, is Maide chaos again The Nature Divine...
Recanted, denounced as The D'Arcon CuNedda
In rites of old Nedward was Dora,
The mystery Ass-Head and donkey in-âne.

Maide similarly anonymous by revisionist new version,
Signifies now, the word ***Laguna,***

‘ A woman of dubious worth ’,
The female whose status remains undefined.
Years. I suffered that.

Were punic slashings, Mère reminders...
By cane attacked at school.
Teaching Phenus Canaan is punished still in Egypt:
And arisen vengeance only, the setting of those people free.
Out of Khem clandestine had they ported stolen formulae,
Star-hung God-Codings guarded by The Hanging God on Yggdrasil Tree.
Who for crimes judged less than this near killed himself,
The Hanging Demi-God become oracular was L'Ædin.

(Seer so cautious for his life,
Did hinge every syllable upon the hint,
Cryptographer Michel de Nostradamus.)

While dream suspended still unravels....
Chancy the bond with second-daughter-child my own,
Perverse her spirit, abrasive. Subversive always.
Facts once privy now intimate told...
To be bruited the familial.

BOOK FOUR

MY MOTHER'S HOUSE BE WILDERNESS

You may recall the Harrowing.
The Harrowing Ap Hall -
Learning first the vetting -
Then multi-ramiffects
Were scarce confined in former book,
Compounded Crucible of Judaspaters...*
Cup runneth over into this one.

Acquitted me pursuit of knowledge,
Eduquieted me they had:
Maide palpbale in the neutral flesh
Had formed assumptions Judas-friendly,
First tiding good, then tiding evil...
The venom was Tod Hall.

Wondrous now, the hollow resignation,

Might make no sense of thing seemed life.
Was there pattern, then to me not disclosed,
Threads proving opposite in fact.
Recognition previous - providence no more than gloss -
Relegated tendril but performing prologue;
Variations on a theme new grapple, vinous subtle...
Progressions compounded and varietal.
So stormy the curtain been first introduced...
How presaged further? dovetailed the plot?

Be-Wilderment My Mother's House
Her Many Storieys, Men in Mansions.

Graduate harmed wrestlings, near flown the coop
Calumbnus slot, cufflings Mother Scooled.
A paper boat life set out to see...

BOOK FIVE

WINGS OF THE DOVE

Noter Damus:

When we toured together; when still we seemed as friends... *
We travelled the western roads through Indian reservations...
Not inundate with tourist then... the habitat, snake and raptor.

And aloof if not inimical...
Did intimidate, the Indian,
No access permitted his silence or remoteness his observance,
Implacable shackled the stilled abeyance
Of government Grant and Preserve,
The imprisonment, pressuring light.

Lordship cruel, the arid land.

A continent sacked and divided.
Horribly plain was union plundered,
Verdure devised martial bounty,
Administered the cabal dubbed government federal:
Rich-fruit allotment gained franchise by blood-cost profligate...
Indulgence was wanton... whole-caust of war.

Shamed, the realization I was hated anglo-prototype,
Oppressor condemned in Indian eyes...
Yet there was accorded me same vision opened Patmost...
Unfurling revelations holo-caustic had overcome the Dia-mansion World:
What if Wasteland promised was long completed fact,
This sterile stretch of earth already delivered of Armageddon?

Endlessness weighing terrible... brazen vault the sullen sky...
Where drifted Tyrannous Scourge its parching spirit
Over sprawling plains dust-suffocate chaost,
Danced scouring of thermal coiled wiccad fandango to woeuver the sands,
Left pitted terrain but shard-strew shatter, its mineral rock...
Witnessed tabula the vitreous dolmen, bone-bleached to whiteness Gilead.

Did what Devil-spawn degrade and pulverize all bounty to micronized ash?
From whence issued winds raising cain wicker'd soils,
Flayed dissipate clouds withholding the rain,
Plunged fathoms burned-earth its incinerate life,
Which secure of no haven, repeated no more?

Harrowed more than hallowed,
The fused and savage burning bowl, charnel his Domain...

Ancient God-Sun Was Apollo the rod chastised intended earthly abrogation,
Assaulted it soon, whole temple the earth:
Flung hurlings incessant his fiery bolt,
Projectile cremating, pierced missile-heads random.
Then abombination of the latter-days, new oracle atomic,
War-Head great waracular discharged its judgement unequivocal:
Pronouncement final its solution:
The rent in the heavenly veil!

It came to me
Great wars had scorched and given shape this place;
Neptune, Venus overcome, and plutonic force deployed by thundering
Solar Deus, more suited name of 'mushroom head' the Atom Fishion King.

Mortal senses not equipped their contemplation,
Systems giant satellite to dwarf the local wanderers long considered ours.
(Yet were coveted far planets; would remain the worlds to die for...
Brilliances to dispatch the future ventures colonised our outer space.)

Great the long red buttes marched Indian horizon;
Lay reaches miles along the ramparts,
Escarpments foundation megalith, battalions titan stepped.

I dreamed of high walled cities, base-footings borne these battlements,
Suggesting spiring skyborn pylons marched unearthly metalled feet -
Trod patterned grids of checkerboard poised in readiness for war:
Titanic mega-stanchions was unconceived their like before.

Came vision of pinnacles soaring, lanced silvered altitudes the miles,
To disappear and dissipate as mists of arcing space.
Beacons were colossi Nephilim, taproot circuits amplified commands
Resonated stellar their transmittal; flung networked oscillating currents
Over cosmos constellated light-years beyond our outermost planet of Pluto,
To further pulse the sky wave, relayed Nephilim enjoinment and directive,
Had Gaulaxics engineered their marvels were the Watch Towers Mag-Daleda,
Lofting modulated mega-frequencies continuous;
Yet not even these were more than secondary outpost,
Housings but subsidiary.
Remotenesses unknowable lain space-time, their mainline central plexus:
Dismissed by us as less than legend, ' The Giant Missing Planet Twelve '.
But familiar to native Nephilim as Magdas Coop of Megda-Lact Gaulactical.

Fantastic fingers preceding Towers of Babel, spiralled cilia hair like...
Arcs where now the network linked Mother-Systems hailing Magaplanet Giant,
The communicants of undivided tongue sparked high-digital Antennae?

The hebrew language still retains its ancient word, ***Magdala;***
It connotes the tower that serves as stronghold fortress.

(Hence Rapunzeloid tale did from beacon hang glorious skein her hair;
Like we are told once laved humble the messianic feet.

Be-witched and harmed at any rate, Our Har-Magedda,
Locked boxed in secret tor by Terrebin Arcane
Imprisoning her against the magic she possessed,
The Potency of Life's creation;
Hated Her, The Magus Real was Magi-Dala,
Would vilify as ' Wicca Witch '
This Priestess sage and Willow Judge,
Who assessing swift all motives wicked,
Could swift with willow wand or broom wreak Har-Magidden of Her own.

{ Though Mes-Sionic notwithstanding,
She sought no candidacy as bride of any,
And therefore Barbered prompt those shining locks
Graced popular saint of fortifications,
Pride of architects and engineers, the beloved Saint was Barbara,
Worshipped long as mystical Venus splendrous crowned Her mountain tower.

Were advised those bon vivants who hoped obtain Her hand,
To provision themselves with suitable rope or coilings of hair
Spun lengths the reach of feet, twelve thousand:
Mayhap enabling so chancy a scaling
Was mounting of the Venusberg. })

* * *

Land set red massif fused. Sculpted the sand:
Glazed the strew of chemical was fired to starkest molten beauty,
To vitrinous rainbow pulverized,
Celestial earth-life phosphorescence pastel shaded.

Could but suggest, such luminous reach of empty plain,
The drenching, bombardment atomic,
But of plenitude designed the scale of galaxies unknown to outer planets.

Well. Clean enough the earth now:
Pale cosmerderm and sterile palette.
Predictable solution to pollution proved pandemic plagues our present day.

Recounts it Indian legend,

Did first exist a world before was Maide this present one...
Cradle quintessential we are told, the origin of man;
Repositor of every grace miraculous, dream handed down as sacred myth.
Yet imprinted and fused in witnessing rock is record to seem more true....

Happenstance was Genesis (the one believed to be our first),
A thing instead remembered...
When America was the prehistoric target, enduring earlier armageddon...
Occurring vanquishment already in those Wars of Revelation.

Age old that assumption sets ***Revelations*** nebulous in some future.
How if it should prove as nothing more than past forgotten was imperfect,
And revenant, old Genesis but ushers in edenic annihilation comes anew?

Pristine withal their appearance, American lands ranging west,
Yet roll proliferate beneath those surfaces of innocent smiling skin,
The installations, systems-nuclear dedicate to death:
Stark predication of the lethal world lain covert, of aspect not so fair.

In proximity thereto and burrowed deep its mountain perch,
Thrived operations, home and community elite the coven was Los Alamos;
Privileged cabal of physicist-priesthood,

Underwritten and maintained by a military indulgent of its scientists,
Oppenheimer, Teller, et al.,
Who contended only feebly with authority accelerate,
Wielded by the governmental agency new all powerful: AEC!
Showing little concern for those abominations that all did duly propose.

Are nowhere cited the Amerindians' sacred myths.
Negating these is nightmare militaristic hades constructed underground...
Housing shuttled missile deployment installation and stockpiled ' nukes ';

Designed computer networked satellites, monitors hovered ubiquitous:
Stashed spent-fuel rods amidst the bursting rodent barrows -
With all related arsenal of poison burgeoned chemical or biological,
Expedited Death, atomized anew The Armageddon -
Prophetic culmination of events,
The past conjoined of future:
A cataclysm known and harsh recorded:
Meltdown Catacomb Praeiudico.

(Struck down and all Her works obliterate -
Was always intended their destruction -
The Battlements of Magdaleda -

Renaming her hence, The Watch Tower of Sion?
Far colony indeed! to so pursue and oppress her!
The Enemies of The Goddess!

New transplant I, in black pool township,
Where was sown the Eyefful simulacrum, Lookout,
Looping sister towers of Collage Des Tours Magdala.
Infeasible the aerial functions catered towerist daytour commerce solely,
Sprung not these contrivances from throwback antecedent,
They were things derived not fanciful but lain collective mind:

Relaying direct to society gone underground, gone covert;
While receiving those Modified Systems Grammaton Cryptos,
All those dwelling above it?)

Nexus shattered, Hill of Migdal. Maide ter-raine oblituary:
Cote of the Dove. Colline H Ar Megiddo.

* * *

Bore mien the bleak resemblance, to those lands surrounded ancient Egypt
Before enriched the soil their coursings, the deltic waters of The Nile.

Counselled by Osiris, mate was her Love,
The son and companion beside her,
Pleasant was dalliance the life lived by Isis,

And seeming the same for a time, life the Queenship, Tiy's...
A regnancy extended gracious to embrace him,
Son and princeling was Akhnatan,
Raising him The Sun-God Mate:
Who in nought deterred the pursuit of heresies unbridled,
For himself would conjure god-identity was more than pharoanoic.

The glory her world was thence anathematized... blasted to ignominy.
A coterie sued relentless, predator priesthood of Amon...
Dispatching The Dove, night tenebrous,

Internment rough chamber the commoner's tomb,
Offered heinous displacement her flesh;
Was DeVinous Blood Sanguine reviled!
Excised forever, The Lineage Tabled:
And anonymous Maide Columbed Derelitta.

To suffer similar entrapment

The Migdal coming after.
Maide obliterate once again her passage.

Praeumbro of priesthood was romish; abbots, inquisitors holy,
Abettors of the abbatoire... avowed its new obeisance,
Murderous maintained it, the implacable status quo:

Pogroms devised by scavengers brutal,
The peacekeepers militant state:
Regurgitant raptors the pristine,
Holy The Piscine Flesh.

Served same god was sadyrgist and sodistgode,
Unslaked the bloodthirst willed supremacy of barbarism
Obtained savage chaos over reason... mercy...
Bred and sent first allies,
Hordes come down from Indo-European enclaves,
Brigand races of aggression...
Assassins systematic crazed, and warshipt linga-mascur lines....

Persuaded through hashish dream they entered priapic paradise unending,
Some indulged hashidic ecstasy roamed frenzied search of prey to kill

By practice of thuggee in deathly worship of the Hindu Goddess Kali,
And the further honor of ' The Old Man ' on his mountain;
Who, in fulfillment of his service, they were fondly led to believe,
Would grant them ultimate return to those ravishments foretasted
When lifted up to the sexual heavens.

Executing by stealth,
Murderer delighting all his prophets -
In the massacre of lives
That celebrated life-enhancing peaceful goddess.

Remember.
Roots intertwine linking hidden assassin (hashish and thatch!).

(Unto this day, hangs remnant thatch is yashmak.)

BOOK SIX

IN THE LEACH FIELDS OF THE GRAIL

Noter Damus

Into the world come child as pauper:
Swathed its attire the poor-laws rank:
Hosted bierghosted, shabby donations old clothing,
Gracious sent government wardens
From district prisons and workhouse.

Even so. Do some progress no further place,
Forever denied the worlds seen beyond them -
Paupers condemned from the first,
And pauper their sentence the end.

Preen-cess Paupress rags and britches
To pine and learn to starve again!
Generosity, mourns him lost,
Shivar Pavarty, Eternal Her Lord....

* * *

So have I forgotten Maman?
No. But the world has me scruff of the neck.

I see the news. I weep. I write.

Viewing Fissure Manq-King Mad on tell a vision world insane
Is shaken to its Hussein-shoes, what is sane?
Gulf the jouffre search out! Satanic pit destroy! and Hit-lerize!

Walled isolate within his husse,
Was he formerly participant or no:
Each embraces his war! Willy-nilly!
Gulphs the bloody gobbet,
Noowse hung his separate ration.

We knew - was all over -
That historic August day - ***When The Fat Lady Sang***
American National An-thumbed vile and base ball;
Latter-day Aversion, low ball Woodstock Wallow Bawl Game,
And courtesy mocked, unpresedentia...
La Grosinante Bahrene erupting fontanelle
In ancient glottal coqapoll iu-pest and satyrsangre.

The world is sceen coalition,
Cloaca pit saytanus hidden in the flesh pit tuit brain,

Riotous mobilizes mob-life.
Koup-weight the coup de mort waged all the world!
Cou-ard phoenixan, redneck bearded burning.
Oh ominous nefastum! Unholy deeds earth's blood abominastim!

Wars within the western world society ongoing:
War in ancient lands phoenicians' flaming immolate -
The Dove Ku-Weight! torched phoenix.

(I too survived the wars plunged desert phoenix on my own
{ And Phoenix Leasing, scam to burn us, lees-singe turn us bankrupt }:
In childhood we had seen a pack of murderous rebels stone a woman,
Pursue her screams through Dublin's Phoenix Park
{ Familiar haunt of James the Joyce come before the Joycie James }.
Wreck-tangled as appeared the dreams my innermost worlds,
As Phoenix-Dove Quad-Wrang-ulele.)

Eternal resurgence albeit, too willing conflagrates the Phoenix,
Rises radiant fissioned ash-rose, spirit weakened, Wholy Nuked.

Recounting again of events as they happen:
Of flying sceen the Miss Ile through outermost Pater-mos air:

Of bombs that dive la rêve invasion wise
From gnatlike planes of war that swarm the desert plage -
Wing fearsome plague to plunge and sting in mechanistic gad-flight,
Asilus kin to terri-locust scourge, first culex-goad the horror vile
Before which Miss Io fled.

Irocquets firing Miss-Isle
(On Our Lady Mother of The Isles!)

Mission theirs to pit and kill all fruit has ever issued from the Stone.
Heap Humaninity on all things Maide were first Her own.

So blessed be the gun-piece-makers!
Terrorists legion, Guns in-errant, Inherantors of Shattain...
Who scorch the verdant earth and all Her School, Ogmayos:
Wither even Her, Madonar Lexis Joyous Alegria, The Cultrix every Gloss.
Comes and stings her, base culex, anorexic son the Hercule Sun-face,
Prompted by Apollo, first supplanted d'Ogma...
Ety'm fruits Her Lexicon was Spiral,
She who was, by Allah! Culexicon Allée Guorred!

Loo-Kowt Wookey Holey World!

Loose! is Sulfurious almost free!
Fair-seeming to his people...
Mongrels wholly oppressed by religious compulsion
Pounded holy hate and terrorisk,
Incited prejudice and bigotry to race riot crazing;
Straitened their minds the brain-thundered men,
Brawlers mad-cracked, street-fighters unruly
The hypnotized polls enamored of war,
And squandering of life...
Ripped from the women who give it.

Arms borne endless service, the mythic Shatein's.
(Countless those swarms exalted the hushein frenzy,
Addicted crack and hashish: Iwrexis crack troops.
{ Troops at home enthralled their same affliction - ours! }

And they will take the world down...
Destruip and drain Her Earth its blood,
Earth Her Body, Oil Her Blood...
To slick its seas the Persian Gulf,
Spill as waste the trackless sands...
Then punitive, bonfire it crude to burn up the air of the world.

Does either scourge present the destiny is feared...
A detainment in soul's earthly hell.

" Watch out you Yankiphulets!
You think you'll buy our domination!
Set yourselves up in our place!
Hate-wished you annihilation! Filthy rich US'ers!
Your greed for oil will bring you into tow the line!
Our fuel reactor breeders spent subdue you,
Prime you Iwreckis' target. ")

Had brought burning water worldwide,
The shemite pyrronoia.
But Jihad holy this!
Some kind of armor-godden!

* * *

Io, The Cow-Horned Goddess. Maman Io-Bocula-Bu-Cephalus,
Gracing Kundige Her presence, millennia hence,
Consoles her, Kundoliores, " **Loo Kuhnder! Little Cow....** "
Cownselling bos-crossing, safe wayfare per-sou-ant of truth.

Despite concurrent times despairilments,
And traumatevil notwithstanding,
Transpires She is not done with me, Mysteriss Maman...

Her Ankhoring Seal, borne circular,
Life-binding imprint, De.En A. New Disc -
She utters the spiral Sound Her Pyotry
As Python Pi-God Magdalen:

As pyot magpie Her own bird,
Limns Her-Ryzons Valley Aridzona, defines dezease:
The symptomatic shortfall rained First Megiddo's Eve
That harnessed atom-symbol of the sun that did prophesy Elijah.
(Where Hail-Airy-Zona once lived Gau-Free .)

*   *   *

They still search out The Stone, Maman,
Why do you require that I write, to thus reveal?
Are You sure? Is it yet one last de-vicing? Another of Your Trix?
What now shall it serve, The Grail?
(War tails thee, Oenclay? Unruly war your burgeoning cells?)

Do You Yourself desire destruction of it all Maman?..
Abandoning cause as lost Dub-ate ignited fire the harrowcane,
Burned volacane the Land of Cain'an Mark of Ham
To maliterre upheaval of blackened earth scorch-martial,
Sent detonate atomic-chaine arcane disturbulast?
I had believed such thing impossible...
(File Yeo-men of England defiling Her Name,
De-faim Her, La Femme! Rank Beef-Eaters infemmous slabbed...
Gorged phagos bespeaking consumption of Goddess and Matrix Primordial,
Most Holy And Peerless... the beef now Cornèd The Cow!

{ Watched his strut sad sorry dam swore cloaca hussyfit -
Sported moustaphake.

Comes war news from the Gouffre by way of pool-reportage...
Communication lackeys, would-be kings of some sort
Gout complaint eternal, slaver squalver prime time
Over revenue the oil wells,
Pools gout the black and liquid gold.
Accursed source of black guerreill uprising....
Is blacquelled soon of course! }

[Blackwell reporting.
With blackstone masonric supporting the bush.
Sprout baronies new cabal networks,
Feifdoms earth-engulfing exact the tithing but another kind.])

Central once, The Garden. Edenic dream thing still recurring....

But abandoned as cunletta, laguna is cunette.
(Remember her: Laguna!)
Lacoon the watery dragon, effluence was delta,
Did mighty Egypt bow before the Horus hawk.

Ate apolo-populi of Apollution, then did revery was Paradise
Underwrite the foraging of Hell.

* * *

BOOK SEVEN

BEWARE! TO'D TRIPLE IO

(Maman)

Editor's note: Italic typeface denotes the speech of Maman.
Regular typeface denotes the speech of Noter Damus (Joyce James).

Golden Trove-Childe, hied the ancient hoard was Castle Hoowarth...
Why weep away your three eyed treasure,
Dream eyes read bloody knowledge at the source of truth is war?
Red tres-yeux yours becomes but nurture wasted
In the rank denuded wilderness where nothing rightly grows but barter
Of flux is Mother's Blood, black rivered gold flows tears trois-l'oeuil,
Pressings of the ancient stone gushed Petra-oil: Oh well!

Oil and s'oil bear food the fruits of earth. Her flora springs abiding.
But genetic formulae world-stock trea-sure devised on the Tree DE.N.AY.
Is by cataclysm sent demanic, flayed to death.
Sheds even macro-world the bloody tears are three-eyed,
Plundered and pillaged by mindless wars wrestled brutal for possession.

For coded tres-yeux will thieves seek you out!
And perhaps you will be killed
By the people stolen from the Maide, made stollen by Apollo.

Je m'appelle always, Io.
(The Fruit Ap Io Pelle derives from tabled Columbes of The Fila Pool.

{ A face is known eternally: The Messager Alegria. Her image reviled.

Is vilified and hated that incarnate Holy Word.
Petrayals Maide Her goriest yahood monster,
Booed as cinavamprick with Her frankenswinish family...

Shown likewise all Her children, Allegore adulterate...
Maide Bad-Noows Broad-Castra by pre-iudic degradation
Is in current estimation: red anathema!
No. Not a leg to stand on: Merry Bonne Allegera Jambes. })

To be swindled. Fleeced, yet skirting the noose...
Remains unknown the neck will hang there.
But must not place one's head inside it.
Must not!

* * *

Oh did Burgess Antonym sigh! The Wose of Joyce (was James),
Desperate his attempt who taught the multi-meaning of The Word.
Yet the Cowde was lost despite him.

Loaned twice my name to whom you bore: Io (Ash-Ash {Isis}).
Hailed Stone Khemicael of Egypt, the first one...

By suffocation dying, cremated thence to Ash Ash... phoenix burned.
Nigh following into death, the Grail.

Then were you designated Hote. Host of Petri House Pietà.
And revealed to you how Dove-tailed together
Those tumblers layered the lexi-locks spelled My Misericodex Descenza.

How then?
(So conyng sly was fyled clef striate

Lock and integer columbed dovecut eunut size to murderous **DOR**
Fit Proteus-like his accommodating bed,
The Wayfarer wracked and stretched nocturnal,
Or rested neatly hacked his limbs to sighze,
On travellers' bed suited all.)

Wayfared My House O'Pain Venêtre.
Where you lay mute same helpless deeps of darkness
Before yielding up last integer locked the gulf was birth and death.

Ill-respired your lungs and throat...
Esophagus gone and wind sore

Gasped fin death's bourne wept pleuronoma:
Knife radical that rolled your stone from sepulchre's door,
Cave-hewn rib-o-nukill where rested solar light,
L'Hote de Vin-Estrus.

Needed good body indeed, our vine;
Venetum was final, intended its last.
Not readily are we overcome my child!
And so we did endure;
Hiding Our secret the heart of the world.

(Less important to whom we are born,
Than is entrance prepared the right time .)

No truth is promised inspiring the world that its leader is coming -

Nought but the ruse attempts rout of remains
That ilk was Maide-laine's:
A line eleminhated almost total
Except for rudiment first genus
Was stripped identity,
Denuded Irishlike:

By its exercise, Apollicy
Declares the world no longer theirs....
No other threat exists.

But yes: the second daughter Io does.

Subverter. Joiner-up of Apollosition,
Informer always of family fact is intimate told
Or is learned about subversive:
Another kind of sainted paull
Damned on the road to de-maskus.

*   *   *

BOOK EIGHT

MARÉE-FREE CREATED SHE THEM

Noter Damus

Women! You breed serfs for men! You breed servants!
You proffer sons as fodder for the mortial maloch!
In cowardly compliance you have done this!

Yet still you fecundate. Conform.
Why have you not refused?

I know well the pressure of ' persuasion ' applied by the Mal-Mal Societ,
But lives in thrall are worthless!
Vital there should be another one,
Maintained by rule less bloody -
The fiat posits Word of Law announced first Ap-Roe-Dit,
Whereby was life, evolving nuance, cherished and decreed.

Its children first bequeathed immortal souls,
Were blessed from world's beginnings,
Then. When all of them were known to be The Mother's,
Bestowed by Her and born of Her caring...
Souls tutored and raised in nurturing birthright,

That knew beauty of love and pride of honor,
Enhanced the compassion arose eager minds.

I understood it too,
When daughters bearing matriarchal names their mothers',
Lack The Blessedness Her Presence, they neither soul nor body wed.

Control of parturition was process ever natural.
Appointed seasonal to Her Ordering might never occur the births too many
By the cycle was protracted and to earth rhythm keyed.
Now so far debased is human purpose
Are civic mobs deployed to Stone (!) abortion clinics,
Wherein staff and women pregnant, are mortally attacked.

Capable of its assay, decision imparts new life,
Woman, if exercised that freedom, is punished for the severance...
Is felled by Stone, ' The Fallen Woman '!

Life?
What matter exist the children rabid and unwanted, wild and random...
Destined denizens of third and lawless underworld
Scrabbling every trumpery conceived...

Their lives squandered wanton... predators ganged,
Outlaw stalkers of the shadow, brutal familiars the frontiers of death?

Authority of ' the street ' their sole instruction...
Influenced by nothing otherwise -
Else that mindless dominion of bodies undertaking soul-less fornication,
The obsessive yet casual coupling.

Mankinds' sexual congress bears no sweetness in the crop its young.
Licensed and exhorted by the current mores,
Ridden by religion odious, advocates and sponsors human population,
To strain it to dementia, Odo's Sub-Urban Pope class.

(Except when curtailed by civil malaise, recurrences random massacre;
Ancient measures that Asia in its wisdom still employs.)

Plagues of War. Pollution. Flood and famine.
Pestilence and drought:
Long set forth in Revelations the visitations these,
Yet is never addressed their primal root and cause.

Bountiful the matriarchies Hers.

World-order ruling familial. Sustaining.
Did share Her golden children in the sanctity,
Within its truths to dwell secure.

Bore The Goddess Herself, Her Children
To welcoming Garden was Earth...
Where would exist no mis-conception:
No rendering of eden over-populous.

But a world has lost its Mothering Deity...
Relegated stuff of myth, Her Golden Age.
Buried beneath its hume and sod, nostalgia.

And should mankind live its life ephemeral,
Still today is proffered recompense:
A concept far surpassing sufficient:
The Soul-Lives lived immortal. Incarnate renewed.

Her daughters weep.
But She alone shall reck the tally, the losses Maide Her own.

*   *   *

Shall be held I speak as oracle my Mother.
Yet put more plain or simple term,

'Tis She does come to me,
Maintains Her Citadel within my house
(Where was hewed the Stone its sepulchre)
Where lies nought about us but destruction:
Duels death The Yama's versus Life.
Yet devises always The Creatrix Her Maia-Trix, simple trick one more.

Maide servant and Deciphearl of Her-Laureas,
She waketh me from the darkness;
Maketh my hand to write by night,
To pen these books devoted;
Wherefore must preponderate the runnings-over ardent,
Fountained poured;
And herald Script Her News right speedy;
Else vanished unremembered.

Before, my Hand was not Maide clean.
Now am I called and have the Write.
Not flown alone the pen traced scripted word of metal plunging uttermost:

The Word Maide tempered steel with which might no one argue.

Blaise'd Wizard blade Her speech, blasé the speech cut keen:
Sword swift flashing swarred delusion,
Temporail dis-astraed,
Spiteful Dieuce Dyiospiter: Apollo-Dionysus-Phoebus!

Believed them fulfilled,
The conditions been wherefore prepared:
She tells me time is meet Go Spell, Reveal Her Word.
Needful and Maide plain these Chronicles Her's, My Mother's:
Not for getting but for giving mankind
Liberation gained knew knowledge....
Soon will be too late....

Yes.
Now will You give me leave to sleep, so beautiful my Mother?

Rolls up Her Wings and bares Her Wrists: Mother of Us All,
Providing instruction for cleaning a soul:
　　A world: a dish:
　　And Xios Post Hume

Delivers a speech in simple: somewhat astounding, a content historic,
Little libellus
Maide Matter-of-fact,
Abreast of the times....

BOOK NINE

B'ACCHURSED HER NAME, HER DIEN.AY

Maman: Not You But I

Maide My goal: Your Ultimate Self to tread its earth substantial.

Despite the compromise of origin. Our shabby, scaly lowliness....
Consider. This birth was contrivance by Me:
Coup the conception Maide energy highest...
Achievement renewing The Day Of My Life...
Defining declension of Daughter-Maide-Image.
Maide prompt Our provision, Maide fitting Our needs.

(Conjure again My School Colline, home of childhood rooted you,
Tutored you, Knoll-Edge holding you....
Circled dreamings Calv-airy Calf was Io:
Where shelves were precious laden, stocked a skull your own golgotha,
Recurring cross the dream of Small Green Hill.)

Well! Now are We familiarized unpopular!
Bowdlerized Our Face and Form:
Anathematized and changed Our Very Gender! Obliterate or mutilate,
Unhallowed held Our Name, or Merely is usurped!
And followed greater ill than that: ***expunged!***

A story everywhere pre-empted.
Bruited yours as well as mine.
We are travestied denigrate and accursed, Maudire!
And world that I devised is stolen from me.

As to the manner of that loss...
Read within these volumes
Of history diverted, revision presented as truth.

May Land Free Mère created I them:
First systems genus Duo-Finn-Ish,
Mat Construction fully Ap-Roe-Dit....
Their appointments in accordance with Efem-meris,
Was ancient astro-almanac derived Our native planet.

Swift the woeving, solid form
Composed the crystal world from singular element borne therein:
Creation's powers were thrust their highest...
Sang each one Our Living Song,

Reached on eternality, endearing themes,
Contrivances not earthly, diversities to explode forever.

Dear that Lord of All The Waters,
Gave His Living Cells White Manna,
Gave the food may not be divided,
Fed the multitude, but did not lessen,
Not even death could bear away.

Sized to a world created new for them, My children
(Still stands in Greece the Stone W'Omphallos commemorates the Gau),
But by inphan-tastes supplanted, the eve-ilk kinder threads philatim,
Was Ladan with his kind seduced:
Tricked coqu-ate Ap Poulay: cuip-trick cuireadh ruester
Tampering gene and chromosome the De.en.ay.
Practual and by pro-pagan-dies.

Then refuted formally true founder, The Lady Goddess Diena was denied.
Overcame Her Deuce/Dyaus/Zeus/Jove/Jehovah/Iacha/
A-Pullatus was A-Poullio was Iupeter/was Ahmmon.
(Aethop blacked by the sun.)

Absorbed, abused, ***cross-bred*** *with other lesser stock,*
Lost to gross corruption was Lux Heifer: his form debased Lu-Cipherian,
Become that principle was Satan. (Anagram: Tanus See.)

First life fulminant opposed it A-pollo;
Intellect-twin had reflected my own.

(*Twisted threads of envy even so, Bacchiccup warpage his mentation;*
Crossing over periodic, those borders pollopathic....
Issued of the gods, his assemblage formed ill-favored was not refuted;
No more suggested bacchurse than the lizard mere grotesque...
Chunk of squatted spore and toad-slick, visage squinted mushroom fold.)
Faced the new familial beauty bore likeness to Our Mother,
Amphibial grew jealous!
Were blasted bitter wintry malevol, Larynxian High-lairy Stock...
Lashed ill-wind to curse and strip them, descendants his sister's kin.

Then growing Col-I gene recombinant, harshest Brother,
By sleight of hand salamantrix, new protocol devised his own:
Carrier streaking mortal plague, dug divot undivine,
Bleak formulae-dioxide-skein, slime-of-skin prolifu-rat:
Sere despoliant shrouded earth m'acc-kine in degradations famigensic,
Quickly rendered ocean's body to famislick of chyme
Parched the soil: mashination burned it desert reach the sterile sand.

But all of that came later... and no snake's harmless milk.

*   *   *

I see no love.
I see no love... its sweetness.
Is nothing otherwise to draw me....

(And yet... and yet....
Do monstrous bear some clause my blood...
Retain aquatic remnants, Bliss their Fathering;
Born the Central Isle was Man's, and glory meant Ladan.)

Some risk to my heart...
I begin my story... yarn unwinding ever was but one,
Rising swirling realms forgotten mists
The origins lain earths beyond all limit known,
But yet were antecedent.

Lest should chance, ladino-mongrelize him too
(Before traduced apprenticeship racqueted battledore and shuttlecock,
The servitor of landed Miss Isle),
I must describe his beginnings first Maide:
What Ladan Steady Hand was meant to be:

Not Diego draco, but the Lookout, guarded treasure,
God aquatic wound eternal river round The Yggr Tree of Life,
Round Seal à Mère calved cheifers,
Formed alphabet the D.En.Ay to make from this Her Mère-folk.

Did Blessed Llyr, The Key Great Llave immortal,
Donate Holy Immortal Cells whence was sprung new Human Life Original.
Non-Clonic Mini-Templete, was L'ove and egg bestowed upon Di'eggo,
A keying of L'oeuf locked fast on Root the Son and Heir
Of Io Hu-Mana Maide D.En.Ay
A new Cell-estril: The First Created Ladan.
Was conferred on him corona our prehistoric Cell-tic names
From White The Goddess Mana Wyddon Everlasting
Who bore The Life His Sacred Cells White Food,
Came Life Le Vie... and Athon of heaven....
(Faulty the legend tells White Goddess Manawyddon is 'Son of Llyr.'
One confounding more: Was Moses sent White Manna in the desert!)

Dove celestial-keeps, accelerate light
Dove from A Star-Terre, Her far-distanced hume...
Sliced fathoming deeps to plumb nephilim...
Ankhor sunk down on the Isles of Man - were sacred domains A-Starter's.

Great was Her labor, Ash-Ash Astaroth.
Were needed fortress-keeps; work-site enclosures to stand Round Towers,
Wherein to remodel Les Oeufs borne Her body,
Ultimate source of L'Oeuvre the immaculate born -
D'Oeuf evolved as Man and Work of Love producing newest bio-being Ladan:
Sprung full grown and huge of stature instructed by egg-dna of Her womb.

(Ladan stems eponymous - from Llavi-Adon.
Spread reach its attribution from Lyons to Caer L'Isle,
And towns remote as Leydon; to this day are celebrated English Wakes,
The Lugh-Mass: Lammas.)

Its life conjoint Grailed Nave Her own pelvic girdle:
Deana Luxipheroahs Fary.
(Or Her Minimized entitlements, Bearer of Light,
Our Lady Diana, who spiralled language Riboneu-Key,
Coded our Life Via De.En.Ay: The Shape-Heard Cheipher Maide.)

Ladaenn Llew-Llaw Cipher-Llews, Lughorfire the Long-armed
(Llyr as Llugh as Hugh and Llud, and Llew Llyr Noden):
Was Bran his beloved and giant son,
Prodigy whose singing head was immortalized in Mabs'n'Ogham.

Serves also as Llew's insignia, the God of doors is Janus;
We see him staring backwards, staring forwards,
Holder of the keys, keeper of the mysteries.
One known betimes as opener of D.o.r.s - on Chaos.

His symbol: Genu Wary capric leaping scales, shape-changing into fish.
Too often is totemic capric-python misconstrued as heir apparent mine.

He is in fact derived the mythos more endemic,
Issue of The Greatest Sea-God,
Most like to Dolphin Flesh...
Who never was woevring dragon!
Unless meant genotype ancestral river,
Winding cells first coursed the Bloodline vanished.

Legends too compelling in their beauty not to hold to truth...
Tales of transformatings Maide La Dia are forever propagate,
According demigods their ancient derogation: ' Tanus '.

(*Yet my jealous twin is male-god, annexes to himself*
All attributes and exploits, prerogative and privilege
Accrued foundation Maide The Law First Femilines

Were Carped from Sacred Cell....
Metes them violence and devicile, matter of course.)

Foundling cast adrift, the child was born of virgin,
Spear-Slinger Llew Lion The Silver Arm,
Llud Llaw Ereint and Lug or L'Hu Llaw Gyffes.
Gryphon antique, the symbol was oldest:
Ruling head of The Lion, his body The Eagle.

We are told was Celtic L'Hu'an deceived....
Conspired against him,
Deu wedded wife, White Olwen,
Full grown was Goddess Flower-Maide Bloodeuwedd,
Fleshed perfection of soft petals, and attar The Whited Blossom's;
Culture her blood derived full the nine trees.

Yet favoring more fondly her lover,
Vengeful, sought the way to kill her lord....

Lain concealment, contrived him then her paramour,
To aim at L'Hu'an the poisoned dart - as though some brute beast buck.
On sighting him, leaped human L'Huan the chase:

One foot set single on its back:
Improbable poised the other, midair,
Bestraddled bestride on the rim of his bath.

Near destroyed him noble husband,
Demigod beyond the mortal:
Not one moment Llew Llaw Gyffes was too quick!
Flew shape-changer screaming, shifted his form to an Eagle.

Long his time concealed in sorry wilderness, hid from haunts of men;
If not fully slain as mortal, were pitiful his wounds.

(Would that present-day hussein
Was by party Ba'ath so-chiall received!)

Shame and scandal! mean strategem devised his death,
But spelled adverse was Blodeuwedd: by enchantment turned to owl...
Unloving of the light and sight of day, shunned henceforth by men,
The magic princess once his wife.
From flouwer lines Maide The Bread her body, Bred and blooded royal.
Yet no communicant grateful,
Charisma acted soul's betrayer more than receiving bread the eucharist.

Less wily. Not so guileful in her new simplicity as wife unwitting,
Appears once more Blod Princess Royal Bedrelbod,
To cause him scant escape again! the near undone,
Al Ladan...
Guardian of Llews'Urna,
Ancient Lamp did commandeer The Geniec Treasure.

(*To ever undermine the woman, burned and hot-spurn Lord Apollo:*
Ungracious did transform her, pythoness his daughter Maiden Dauphinée -
Clad rough bark and wreathed its Laurel condemned her stay of poetree.)

I have listed some of those, his names, The Ladan:
Become his state, dark angel doing penance...
Pyth-onoric dragon yoked his service human-kine;
Tanus Maide protector in manner much as Bran, The Giant Head Oracular.
Yet gone untallied the name that is Mine:
Gau Maide Gouffre, the Gulf; Maide the Abyss and the Pyt.

De-Luged the flooded waters, did oil then de-Luge The Wasted Geo-land.
***Luge** becomes the synonym for warfare,*
Earth is freyed and fought about.
Daggers piercing desert shores. Daggers in the sand.

Perceived its degradation did grieve for Her world, The Maide.
Compassionate then companionate with Ladan would nurture him the aeons,
Encourage him in furtherance of his consciousness,
Every symbiotic skill and wit exert to skirt the devastation
Wreaked Her world Apollo Maleficus:
God Tor-Mentor Infortunium. Luckless Death.

Acc another name of goddess Maide Ladan Lord Inheritor Al Ladan's Cavern,
Ludicus once joyful, Lusus naturae.
But Ludus Lingua, lingam lugubrious now. Lugeo Lucifugus...
How easily would A Paul Onion make him cry.
(By parlay black cock pour-lay, oh phoulaye Ap Io!)
Was by A-Pollo, the Ladan seduced.
Was by Apollo The Ladan reduced to lowly existence pythonic the worme.
Ac-cursed and hypnotized his golden mind, gold was undermined.

Did bury DNA its treasure, Acc. Codes crypted deep within the grotto.
Flesh Maide wholly Word obscured and lost spelled Al Ladan The Avé Saga.
Mystory mentions him subject not much more than Ormis-Worm
Girt lumpish coils of serpent slept his tree:
Weighted down sad mythos, Apollo's bequeathment to him,
Eating only of the golden appols of d'espairides.

Were celestial portals Ia Nus' shut...
Stone was closed the Janus hinge...

Sealed for aye, the oaken doors on House of Lug.
No more lived White Hlaf Bread nor augur-oak hlaf fish.
Once crowned Quernus Q're, now to languish druid loaf-mass - Lughomass.
No more to hear the query, offer up his answer, golden augur auricle.

Nor did Arthur Britain move to aid him (the one who had fathered Bran!).
Possessing in a not so distant future, the prison settlement White Hill.
Was but fitting should become synonymous with dread,
Ravens Apollonic flying black round white His London Tower.

So tell me where is auracle bread? Is in the ear or in the head?

The Ladan walks amongst us still...
Tinker, taylor, coffin-board maker.
Mother-Son religion reflects the tragedy recurring
A-Paulonion Oracular the Jesus line.
Goddess-Wife not Mère usurped, but Mother-Goddess removed!
Does he know? No. Not yet will he first attempt the Lammbas role,
Redeemer Son despairing original sin.

Chants Mourning Dove her Requiem. Reminiscent. Désolé.
Lamenting archetype, first begotten kinder,
Crowns worn suc-cessit tanus incarnation,
Father of them all the Ladan...
Capered scapegoat nailed self-immolate to impotence his wooden mock.
Crucified and good as dead, the Kuhndalin.
(***Maidened by Apollo in much the same de-manner***
As de-headed healer-tanus Aesculapius.)

Yet should Humeskin balance python scales:
Long reptilian taile be shed - and stifled coils no more the spine
Its dual caduceus, caducity inflicted issue mortal,
Same narcosis overcoming L'Adam, to which young Endzymion succumbed,

Then shall come again old Eden.
That Eden promised and is foretold.

(Not perhaps that fullness blessed before, yet will not come its end.)
Scale exists beyond the spatial, beyond the scaffolding called time;
Where flourishes lineal thought no further,
Sequential past or future,
And seems cur-tailed the Laedan shackled history sprung Edenic span.

He shall be cradled stele, and nurtured,
In Delphin Stone The Gau Omphalos, navel of the world,

But come as Ladan Wholly Child,
Infant First of All the Living:
Sprung not complete in semblanced manhood, derived cerebral formulation,
But felicitous and cyclical, those developments accorded human children.

(Attribution further, wholly false:
That emerged Athena the cerebral caeli, swollen vault was Zeus' head.)

He shall attain his Mighty Sonship,
Stand Guardian of The Tree of Life is rooted springs are crystal-eyed,
Wink as rivers serpentine meeting oceanic deeps
Where silent glides Le Viathan eternal,
Vast looming plunges living wake the delphic sway.

All colossus scale successful shed,
He shall receive again the Living-Cells
Make such genesis immeasurable;
Himself the Capric Goalden Fleece,
Melon-Gene is Child of Ram and Ladan Golden Fruit Immortal.

Reduced him Minne-terre: Maide Avé-nus.
Dedicate once more and full composed Great Ladan,
By His Lady, Deyenné.

*   *   *

Benefit promised that:
Now shall I explain what is signified to ***you:***
Recapitulate the facts are salient....

First Kuhnder-child new seed awaiting his completion;
Maide and bore him, Ladathean,
Threadings Dienae The Living Tree was human spine columnar...
And Holy Cells Divine transplanted,
Indulgence came Immortal Leviathon.

Yet by the Apollo felled and tempted.
Head turned and undermined with words so soft were trusted sympathetic,
Counselled was his life but sentence spelled enslavement...

' *And as to truth and purpose of humanity its existence, my dear!*
Was maide but singular machine performed the labor gathers up the Gold!

Well may you wear the fleeting semblance... contrivance of your maker;
But abused and overworked it, falls dissolute the frail and mortal body;
No longer useful digging goldfields,
Proclaims that you are old....
Slave designed for obsolescence, is then by death disposed!

Yes! young friend and nephew! Could I lie to you?
Not of death have you learned, it is sure,
Yet this is the plan she intended.

Do not believe my scurvy sister bitch has any further niche for you.
She carries and cares for naught but our seed!
Derives it from us! The human race.
No glory there! but tanus de-manned to her bidding....
They milk us of seed: use us as bondsmen to broodmares maternal.
Render us castrate inferiors in Woman's World!
Yet almost in place, Women Rulers.... '

Anger smoldered, listened.
Already strove contentious, the soul was incomplete;
Vied with Maide about her business, of which he knew so little,
Feeling only sorely vexed as thing accounted less...

Assented ignoranus heard such cock and bull the treacherous counsel:
' Follow this my bidding: you desire to remain as a man!
If you wish to stake your freedom,
Avoid venal plague as you can...

Bite instead these golden apples, eat and swallow the juice their meat:
Then! do you live not to die!
Time enjoyed is never-ending, disports immportal much as I:
Grants you riches, second, third, and omni-sight...
Pleasures of love unknown to mortals. '

Thus Ubhal The Apollo Aphagodic:
Snake proffered of himself!
The one and only Apple! The one and only Snake!

Abol-aoigh did take in hand and tutor Ladan
(Child first one, Maide Diana Io: Horned Goddess Milch Cow Bolaoigh)
In partaking of embrace: the Eating of the Phago-Tree:
Bullocked Cock-Apoxed The Ritual Grecoque wreaked Abominne.

Step the first: to brink the chasm led his death,
Dragging with him every human coming after.

Metamorphosed to predator, affected cults the slaughter sacrificial,
Did kill and eat these harmless beasts compose our own organic skein.
Flesh from tree was conscious life - Mannas Cells were lusted after...
Destined meat decayed. Wormeaten strife. Lives terminal our mannakind.

* * *

Condemned, The Ladan.
Sad creature tangled quest and quarry,
To drag persona, orobourous coil the serpent-worm.

Subjugates him Diabollo, his Un-maker,
Presses him the skills and protocols accomplish abolition of her works,
The Lily Tree....
Introduces worship basely venal of mankined mutants, seed Maide null:
Of Deities stollen garland hung entwinement
De'N.Ay The Gau Tree...
Grafting befoulment on to it, mutilating it.
Removing living keys from it....

Lily toiled the Field, conceived and spun whole tapestry was earth:
Her work Abollished.

Enters time-space into Mini-culture, Ladan.
To evolve from devolution - may one so term sad process, progress.
He will co-mingle, their progenitor, with devolving human hordes,
Victim down-spiralled no less than are they.

He will undertake to first redeem himself,
Agonize imperatives that merciless propel him to attaiming absolution...
And by achievement such, reclaim them all.
Entwined and hooked slow grapple of slippery coil his soul's ascension,
His return was ever destined... the partnering son of The Lady Diana.

Arose new race Divine The Egg, and annointed princely title,
Cosseted court-tanus, Di-Eggo was Lordling highly valued
When removed: his head.

(Its usage consultation; for consciousness retaining every gleaning,
Those particles Maide original DNA.)

A medium proving article of choice for every savage rite
Now exercised on others,
Created them the Heads Oracular sang the song Sa-Tanus;
Fundament invoking lunit, was cherebinth Di-Abollo.

Did Goddess never end the life of mortal tanus as antiquity has claimed,
The legend serves but brother's vengeance,
Maide repositor of his hate.

Is Diana our Sonne. Our Sound.
Her Light but reflected, Apollo...
Dweller the pit and the crater, facophony wailing his moon...
Stronghold fled lunatic spirit, their bailiwick hausing,
Wicca'ed his wights.

Pholly that phollows Apallo! Pall-bearer of humanity.
Pha-goatry the initiation first enjoined, to thence become habitual...
An appetite devolving murderous arcana able in the Cainabal-balistics.
Degraded is The Goddess Culture, become but death cult of the Beast.
Promises mine were meant to keep achieved the ends but butcher's block!
Oh, was inception that easy, the devouring of Our Flesh.
Now does human life's succession depend upon addiction to its blood-lust.
This! is how accomplished the genus' dissolution.

Integrity had seemed such sure appointment -
The genes my planet's carbon seed-stock. Hah!
Jennets Maide the Black Pool! Onagers reconstructed à la A-poolonian.

I remind you again of agelong measure,
Time's bounteous count enjoyed Nephilim -
Wherein does single week approximate allotment human life span...
Amounting earth-cycles the years threescore and ten.

(Intent on fission,
Sent father of Los Adomb-Bombas his myrmidon kamikraze
To explode the teller winds of hell unleashing radiation
Incinerated web organic life arose its soil: a-tombé'd!
Breached it vicious, the Femmi-skein new earth,
Against it sent deployment of de-vice
Dispatched by latest Fission King.

{ Not Maide same device the Adomb-bomb, as Maide A-Damas Bambas. })

Familiar attending Apollo the raven, and deadly lamia occult is the owl.
The scavenger raptor, invention his.
Animal-stealth fed carnivorous.

Silent the hunt, paces predator pack,
Blood thirst the succor his wolves.

Beasts ever roamed free 'neath their own open skies,
Glorious the tracking for helicopt-hunters!
Those sportsmen ennobled by guns, telescopic:
Game herded panicked, stampeding before them -
Hopeless the flight from the deafening scream of hovering chopper -
Random rains slaughtering bullets delivered their heavens, new earth.

To rate almost as high, the sly use of horse.
Great herbivore's scent is deceiving...
So guileless the prey! Disarming it fatal! One timid and Sacred to Dia!

Co-opted La Mare in the slaughter.
Creature is gentle... given my name.
Oh Shame! Mean spirit. Deprauverty!

Visits Apollo on mankind, diseased plague of rodent,
Ravening gut-swarm the locust;
Sprayed is all plant life acidular poison,
Food crop falls blighted, a ruin of miles.

Targets ubiquitous dart-sting,
Insectile injecting its concentrate venom.

And bred is intrusion microbic,
Lofts meltdown sulphuric as gasified cloud-rot.
Varietal virus de-sign-ed ever new, old Trompe DeVil's apallowed death.

Death dispatched vicious and sudden,
Spongelike those tissues eroded by fevers of phagocyte-fungus
Billowing dust epidermuck. Rot-blown Apollen diseased.

Pesticides genetick hybrid.. are phantacides vaunted! truly noxious...
Structured cocktails who knew alchemical what!
Decoctions venal do but reinforce the pest immunity...
Brujo brews ensuring homogenocide.
Breached the codes, My Dna.

Appearing next sardonic mimick, travesty the new Apolproxy Phago-Cide...
Inimical were programmed phagocytes re-routed...
Metastasized the ichors... clawed bitter tooth the chancy phago-cyst...
Sardon-co-noma devouring wholesale, The Appolman's creatures' lives.

(Phago-bio cells amok, atomic geo-world bombarded:
*' **What ails thee? ' Oncil? Oncologous cancern?***
Ancestuous Anfortas. Foretaste of For-satan Maide sans testes?

No friend the Userpent Fissure King to Family of the Grail!

Wizard penilized, sang ros-signol the singer now bloodied red castrati.
New Fishion King, does Klingsor carp and parse his chant all time as one
Had once embarked adulterous upon incisterus...
Who hobbling smitten thigh, incessant thence pros-teste-d.)

Lines derived the bloods true blue were reconstructed,
Carnivorous patternings grafted,
Were instincts predatorial imposed on my sociable ape.
Forever debased, new creature blooded was latter-day ape Ap Apallo's,
Baboon backside issuance a blooming murk of cyanine blue.

Carnifeckless, ultimate his subsumption!
Conshumern degraded to abort-in-carnal.

Bred to blood lust rampant, human carnivores beget immoderate,
Their multitudes proliferated long term, saturate the planet,
Scrape and rape the earth of riches, leave noxious wasteland
Slides erosion leaching ecologistique dust bowl. Toxic.

Stalks them easy plunder: Apolanimos Carnignorass,

Carnivex set down calamitous in the grasslands,
Habitat was peaceable,
Contained the grazing creatures,
Simple herds are gentle and domestic,
Trod they hoofed or cloven footed,
Kine are held precious by Me...
Provisioner and protector of security their existence.

All on a bountied summer's day in Eden...
Was life each one, devised herbivorous:
Sent forth the sheep and lambs clad warmth their wool,
Grazed placid the cows proffered milk;
Built her great strengths the mare hauling transport,
Or for travel and carry, alternative saddled....

Oh... not alone organic food sustaining them, Hu-Manna Kind,
Except as fed delight.
Yet mocked was bounteous Grail dwelt eden...
And Ladan, first fruit of the garden.

Turned him into weeping dragon, Apple-Onion,
Hung him minion on the Ash-Ash tree

Where gold was fleeced... then persuaded it had been his own.

With mythic fruit was tempted, touted as the golden apples...
Being eaten... feeds d'espairides.
How else consume The Tree of Life...
Except contests its maker,
Strives possession of the prize forever Maide desecrate?

Throughout all time, worn every guise, is Ladan lackey to Apollo.

The Italian Tintoretto comprehending,
Painted incidents defined it well:
Tableau, ' **Temptation of Christ** *' in his wilderness...*

And graphic and expositive, truth that lay behind climactic legend,
Ceremony was cryptic, forever obscured,
His ominous ' **Last Supper** *'.*

Thirteen are seated round (another) table.
Gradation scarce perceptible slides from seeming individual to the next;
The aspects epicinematic predominating gathered faces,
Are all of them but subtle variation on Apollo's own.

Spectacle hosts this son his banquet.
Magdala is depicted supplicant on Her knees.
Serving ritual of beliefs disparate, does each one proffer wine or food;
Symbolized by both as transcendental offering,
White The Cell, The Daily Manna.

It is ever maintained was disciple John,
The most beloved by Christ.
Truth errs in this. For John was held in no such case.
(No, nor he who was brother to Magdalen, gone by the name of Lazarus.
{ Shown poignant is his semblance to that sister. })
Presumed esteemed beyond all others, to the extent of seeming revered,
Was Dove Migdala: thought mother-priestess figure idolized.

Mated with the male-child who yet is Her own.
He will father albeit, Her children,
While is brother to them all.

No Last Supper this one. Nor ever was the first.
No Matriarchal Tabulatus honored here,
Shall no perfect fruit of vine be pressed.
Are overturned the tables on Columbnar genealogies;

And overcome within her life, her natural heirs
By traducements came the many arks and covenants,
Spelled sly device by testament was vaunted new,
Affirmed of life eternal - its arrival following after death.

Her son to designate his corpus, eucharistic bread...
Ritualize his flesh in verbal substitution.
But Magdalen alone bears food is served from holy graal.
Is to her Substantiation granted... to host original living cell La Vie,
Subsisting human soul eternal, provenance came Vie Aton true.

Rough-spurned by militenet spurring Apomale,
Revelation stuns, how much she is despised!
Child The Holy Manna Bred!

Despite rebuffal suffered at the hands of factions maschule,
Constellates her, Tintoretto,
Stellar-Center foreground.
Abiding hence for all time, Maide appropriate his homage.

And in mystical temptation, does wilderness darkling proffer him Stone:
Son to usurp: advised the conversion to bread.

Tintoretto knew.
Does Apollo darken Light.
Smite it blind, the soul!

Thing never his The Stone.
It did reside the Magdalen,
Miraculous The Grail...
Reappeared the living Tree Maide Sounding-Stone.
Yet was pre-empted Sonnguine title hers,
Legacy descending from Chanteuse was Creatrix.

And attaching further attribution for himself,
Adopted former name of sister-twin was Phoebe.
Borne that trophy his thereafter:
New Phoebus-was-Apollo.

And abusing over-Laden obscene plot,
Used her name for all time the usurpation greater,
Was Holy Acca-Mater.

We know Apowellow as the serpent twisting sexual
Wrapped the Appol Tree.

(Inhabiting her form a second child dispatched to daughter of the Grail.
Young body twisted similar
By the genetrick draconian...
Afflicted Cerberus Appalsy.
Carries Bac-cursed seed the Apollonian,
Known Iophemistic, Io's Genes.)

Loose-Cifer Rex unrepentant.
Wrecksus unrelenting,
Royls in laughter defrecating water-ladan god the dragon.

Now a power low and fallen,
Had known Apollo high estate.
Never conceded, his envy of Ladan,
But strung the weft its downfall,

Heva-nly cradle was Garten of Heaven surrounded the tre-e'd.en.a.
The Life Maide by Efa was Eve,
Within House of Life was Eva's Eden.

For saache of gold will he f'orsake,
Make of the sacred murderous mock in massacres called Holy Q'War-els;

Afflict by sack beiquitous.
Seek even qu'orey mines the gold my head!
In hope of rule this w'or'ld by voodwar domination over me...
And Ioracular use that head! Vooe-D'Io if he can!
Imposing on the world foundation Maide good bonned
His cock-apock a-pollo,
Head and Minne'd, Maide servitude false Father.

Ladan hangs the gallus:
Gallows hung, are beauteous children persecute.
Not Maide complete or ready the heifer-boeuf:
Oh misfortune! he should work unguarden.
Nor Maide Her Acca, full Ionian soul for Ladan,
Appointing him only within the record set Acc-Ashic stars.

The primary goal was accomplished:
Then by Apollo alas traduced, the Techn Llo-gaum.
Tachen covenant New Logauw Ladan,
Transformed to servitor of lesser worlds,

Logos meant fulfillment would embody Gau Purus,
The Code-Stone worth was Ladan's.

BOOK TEN

THE MANNA CIPHER KEY

Fallen swift the bread new risen...
Sprung whited radiance M'ana's Issue,

Apollo and his 'Lute' *pol-lutes the planet,*
Loots the earth its heritage
Of creatures weaving soul-skein
Maide Her corpus living Goddess.

Communications sent by beast-oraculate included scorpion to serpent...
Animal heads converted to the use of terror-binary.

Wisdom such, distilled zootic,
Was delivered first from Egypt,
Then extended usage further,
Spake his Grecian will, the Delphic God.

Thus peaceful Cell-ts My own are weaned from pastoral pursuit,
Transmogrified as tragic carnibore:
Transfixed its thrall, occult bewitchment
The Cult of Talking Heads.
Surpassing genocide of Genesis, equated geno-Cease!
The Low Apallow's murders.

Comes New Maide Di.N.a each century.
But by Anti-estrus twinned as often! Antagonist Twist....

Intending immolate her heart,
Sends her evil life-dream Baal-Goad DNA:
Baleff Goat is Pan Demonium!
Horribilis est!

(Capric Potence littered chambering cave the source unseen of Jordan)

Pronounces baleful,
' ***Kill or cripple, Whore-ibilis est...!***
Or on Hell-Hound Bacchursed bitch
Let Cerberus get her A-pallsied child!
Ilk Secondilled, lurching Cundrie!
Io (slut co-opted), Quarliario!

At any rate smite sillibate! Crack its fragile temple,
Child twisted, listed, seized what horror!
Better yet! Dispatch it to another Abydon,
The comfort come Fourth-Massiter,
Head living Cerebilis! Dead-icate Ad-Libidos. '

Gravominous Maldit Annunchate Apollo....

' ***Ah. You! that died!*** '

La Demoiselle and Child-Essential
To circle noose was hung the wayfare centered,
Drawn the quartered playing-fylde
Whereby was triple sown the circled dream -
Not fairey taile:

Destined instead des-sues paine due,
Dogged Feyt Matins Laimentenants the Wander-Lust House...
Massiters Hereto Fourt were not all known,
But Maide parallel equation micro-history,
The blood-tormentors of her macro-world.

* * *

I say that Ladan slept.
Awake, asleep.
Who might dream cocqette Apoulys
Was ploy arrayed against him,

Bred new-phallen... eaten Appol!
Oh! should not!
(Nor would any other, but chaldrune devil-spawn was his,
Wreaking history iniquitous, blood-studding as I speak.)

Vessel was but partial, foul seduced Bi-acchus,
Put to use I-Accus! Perverse the Dyon-izeus.

Active entered him the service, Great Qu'Orror W'Haurus red and bloody;
Then restricted him to south of Aur'Oub'Aurus,
Land of Dragon W'Orm could eat but may not think.
Land, reserve of fleece and laden oil black d'or,
Where like worm could dig the soil for gold;
Like pig, his master's truffles.
In Apollo's Aden abattoired,
Shears **himself** *of fleece auram!*

Sacrets hers alone,
Maide Goddess Head contained the world and all which was within it;
Created D'Ora gold the mined does use it.
Is fabled brain-pan, gold sought hermetic, due process frees the maze.
Ore pins the tale the donkey D'Aura, unkind, like blind man's bluff...

Transforms a fool already rich in gold to king of midden-ass base metal,
His assay's ears a gift may never be curetailed...
For only assay spoken true may flood its cells the spine,
Replenishing The D'Auris, Golden C'heifer keys Her gold.

' *Give me! Key Cipher, nuclésecret token-key, new Ribonne Set!* '
Saeth worshipper the Dora.

Pan Daemon-Eon lives, imm-ortus life -
Confers with friends high places,
Loosed and fallen spirits all, the famil nefilim:
Head bowed before its contemplation,
Tree is Root of Life Dimension;
Will read its book the language newly known.

But not wholly can be tachen,
The Life, Diana's Tree.
Was ever so....
Yet seeded Laden fruit-baum
Girt about of dragon coil, as well might useless be....

(*Bomb sleeping and inanimate, or struggled conscious to be free,*

Benefit withheld in either case -
Bad as if the means were gone,
While sacked orobbed the world Black D'Auram which was the Ormeuz blood.
By common belief did means of war aford a crossing to im-ore-tality.)

Had brother besides Phoroneus, earliest Io, remember:
The Hundred-Eyed Pan Optes Set false guard and keeper to betray Her;
Help deliver Her metaformacide,
To shape-change her Ultimate Cow.

Dropped splay of hoof, beast-consciousness amock,
Forded Boss-Phoronean the heifer-wit,
Hauled the Keys of Gold were Io's:
Four-footed thundering panic circled back Her cow track thence to Egypt,
Carried there the Precious Gold Fyles, Leben D'Ore
Derived Columbnar D'Oreich Spine
Connected earth and sea and heaven one,
Endowed typhonic sonars the certainties not mortal:

Provender prodigious, Immortal Cells the deep;
Same genus gift was borne ancestral Undae
Who shared Poisseidon Oncle.

Chronicles do but joke that pose the riddle
States Iocastra was the sphoenix!

Be three, the number Be Atreydes.
Bi-sex Orphanus, be Mère Io-Ponymus Tree betrayed!
And sly will like betray descendants Egypt, House Epaphos,
The sable, somber Ay...
Brother of the Renenet housed soul the Queen was Tiyi,
One did term himself as ' Father of The Killer Son. '

Thought him Oedipul perhaps,
Proving Ay no simple Father of The King.

(*What Ayls thee Ankh-ill?*
Hast lost thy clef de vie?)

Aye! Destroyer of the children all, that far-flung progeny was Io's.
While Set! His ass ears!
Earlier had murdered there, Osiris!
Dissenter was dismembered over gold fields!

* * *

(　Celebrities' recurrence reinkarnak:

Bedfellows stranger never seen than merger countless-eyed TV Panoptes,
Deci-Bull Medea Vict-Ore Deci-Mate and U.B.Wicketous Bang-Ore Mines,
　　　TV Jacqass S. Rauckass,
　　　Mediacrity turned on yes! old Ass-Head Set!
　　　Donkabraxos de-lewds a-bray-sive.)

Drawn ever nearer danger T. Vidangeur, victim herded Mind-Set T. Vid-Io.
　　　Itself economy and ill-omened prize, is fleeced the fleece!
　　　Apo-liced crawls world-skin squalor-warrel...
　　　Upheaved, is short directed:

'　Take this ram-kin treasure reincarnated life and stuff it!
Give me gold immauracle is bred! Not the heart unconscious reinvented!

　　　Oh! Must get me Head!
　　　Re-Medeam's latest message!
Who controils panoptim-eyes, my friend, gains controyalty the world!
Life's biggest boon bestowed! is medium remedial, Vanquisher of Apathy.

Are easily overlooked decaying corpses, images moving to seem as alive!

Well, a form of immortality.... '

(*And gold earned, near Maide its purchase,*
Arc-heifer held last secret: Goal was Goal'd New Man,
Stronghold Golden key of D'Ore to Life is Set the death beyond,
And I'a'mortal!)

' *Listen hard but once Oraqtes!*
For I am Medea, more clever than you!
Given my world the fleece was J'Son!
I stole for him.
So do not try to steal from me!
Remember what his fate!
I could never afford to do it again.
Those children.... '

Love for Golden Maman transmuted over centuries;
To love of Mammon metal gold debased.
Turned on madness. Fished with golden hook.
Equates no more than hunger desecra'd
The Holy Longing for One's Mother,
Now **Maide Execrat-Io!** *Accursed.*

Makes mocks with further pun, the cruel A-Pollo,
Enslaves and keys them, lowly diggers after gold, seed of Golden Ladan,
When was First Father repositor himself the Goal!

* * *

Who knows the good, is forced acquaintance evil;
The polarizing threat confronts all life;
Of chancy-mix proportionate, regenerate, degenerate,
To struggle dominance ever after, rife.
May great suffering sometimes forge connecting link,
Provide at least its vision, wholeness;
As do perhaps selected drugs,
Howbeit is enlightenment all too fleeting.
With circuitry redirected,
Does also sexual force command abeyance
Of imperious will the flesh.

Yet such knowledge requires one grow within it slowly...
To be fed but the line at a time....
Not implanted whole, imparted all at once:
Luminant must form within you,

Organic sunburst fanned alight
To blossom new cognition...
Attaining transmutation extrait in the flesh
Reveals the truth of Holy Chalice, Holy Grail.

Might no-one re-create the world, for that had I made perfect.
And eidolon sublime was intended as Hu-manity...
A conception embodied the qualities proper.

My task to bear all life Myself!
Accronymistoric genes evolving-scale
Set alphabet demarcate on its scalpel shell;
Then hip and cradle bearing-bonne, First Maide The Venus' Chalice.

Had seemed a world enough for you to rule.
But the fated Self has become its shadow.
See how surely all are drawn the rim of vortex....

Clutched you once, would never let you go...
For you I seek safe overlook from seethe and boil of cauldron's bore,
But protection overcome and unsuccessful,
Begets adversity penaltimate.

BOOK ELEVEN

LITTLE PRI-MERE OF THE GRAIL

Not the first and not the last, Gilgamesh...

Same threading story loops all time....
Yea. Unto present day.

Seeker after boon conferred immortality,
Performed the acts of faith would grant him human life forever,
Beseeching Living Breath Her Holy Copht,
Only to show him The Way.

Clairlux In Cephalus Diana Luciferous Soluna Moon-Cow Cipher,
Luce cipher spiralling head alight - nymph immortal was Io;
Carrier of The New Co-lexus hornèd moon.

The brothers hers, Phoroneus
(Fearne was giant, or Tanus Bran)
And Argos Panoptes, Hundred-Eyes unsleeping...
Focused all objects their tracking,
Scanning synchronic the zoo-mar pan-vision.

Suspecting dalliance of Jove with Io,
Single daughter-nymph of River God Inachus,

Did aggrieved and angry spouse, Olympian was Juno,
Detail Pan-Optes Argos, the watch upon his sister....
But by farsighted tactic, sly sleight of hand was Jove's,
He was lulled to sleep, false Argos,
Charmed harmonic airs flowed Hermes' flute....
Confounding in that manner, those charges brought by Juno.

Still protective of his light o'love transforms her Jove, quick magic
To a white and docile, dumb and speechless heifer.

Juno then retaliate passed sentence on the luckless lookout, Argos -
Plucked out those hundred eyes condemned as contumacious,
Contemptuous cast them new adornment gazed the tail of her pet peacock.
But received him next, bad quisling brother,
Atrocity surpassing came the hand of Hermes,
Who ripped the blinded head of Argos from his torso.

But thankful loosed was heifer!
Goaded albeit by gadfly sent circumam-boeulate the globe;
Electing Magi-chorns Ucopian to accompany her,
Protect her from a souris tong that cursed her beasted atavistic -
Epithet deployed first time within Olympian underworlds.

Forded cow bossy, Boss Sporus....
Stampeded the Pontus Euxinus.

(*Water nymph bridging Her pontus:*
Ioxinus, was lain the Black Sea.
Yux! *Eux and Yeux! Stung Iox bossy!*
Eyes circled gadoue'd, bled sewergeyes!
{ *Efflux washed same slippage underfoot*
That noxious gouted culverts poured sea wall,
Pooled Blackpool's slimy strand its sewage. })

Fled the charges Juno's,
Pursued and voiding terror,
Left it mud was ever blacker, inland sea the Euxin.
Cowed in fact and legend is she locked and blocked that speechless form.
Reduced! Once their equal, Maide less than any were familial.

(*And what the source of gene pool created Aethiop?*
Oh. Cowed how easily, people!
By cow-de is divided their speech.
Consigned to Caer Glass Vitr E'en Gloss Castle.
The House of Many Paines!

How now high pontus pontiff pauline triple crowned in Black Unholy Cee!
Pontificates proliferate and overpopulate pollution....
Crossed Fish and Bull encycli-gulling world! How dared you?)

Heifting Key and Talisman, The Io Moon-Horned -
Fulfilled her known world-circuit and reached to Egypt,
Thence restored to former shape and physiognomy the Io-Nymph,
Delivered there her child by Jove...

Entered into marriage with Telegonus she was grateful,
And with that son Epaphus was to found great house served sacred Isis,
Adorn him with Uraeus, The Diadem of Goddess as Maternal Heavenly Snake.
Honored him further - installed him Apis,
The Bull her son was King and Royal Egypt.

(Depending on house you inhabit - and frame of moon you see through.)

Would secretly bear same magikeys and ceiphers from the Pharoah's Egypt,
Jacob and his Sarah.

Benefits those to prosper Israel...
Espoused the cause diaspora.

BOOK TWELVE

WAY FAIRING THE GRAIL

Timeless is our Mode of Travel in Field of Being Comprises Your Space,
Spinning cosmic spindle.
Ship Astarta's, proportioned new necessity, looped the fields elysian,
Adjusting lesser space-time-span, entered random point the globe
To rest in upper Egypt, Land Al Khem,
The ancient city Thebes, gone by former name of Wose.

(*Not! the mythic Greek Thi-vache was situate east Boeotia,*
Renamed to honor echoic, the metropolis Thivai....
Treats legend howsobeit of Oedipus and fratricide,
Of incest, House of Thebes....
But commuted first that tragedy from covert source
Was House of Pharaonic Thebes,
Expunged and overlain the centuries,
All signs erased its quelling... of Royal Egypt.)

Building there symbolic image beast was Holy Sphoenx and Phoenix -
Her prefiguration, Ty of The-Bes.
Widely honored Cooween was Tiye:
New daughter Lady Rib of newclear life,
New being stamped by Ankuh, come again,
Then sealed with Key and Lock of Life.

Maide reincarnate latter Egypt,
Merey-Bonned The Two Horned...
Transcending the ranks of privileged commoner,
Did swift assume the mantle of Mère Cow Holy...
She who was Hote, our Stella Vestalis.

(*As had long ago the Goddess D'Agon, Serpent-tailed,*
Flown comet trailing feathered wake on ship's descent
That passaged Far Awai-Fair Aphrodite,
A crest sometime worshipped as A Star Ti,
Or Crescent Horned The Hathor
{ *Heifer-Aether, Kuh-Wean Kuh-Nome* },
Magi-queen attended by her creature, Hare Nome:
Coney Harelding Vendus News Good Ti-ding anew.)

Grace of Egypt,
Dame built Rib and Fundament of Life,
Again was come new Key-Stone.
She it was would furnish genealogies the original Maere-Vellus:
Tables Stella Maris created Sacred House Ap Aphis,
Cow-ded spiral Io-genic ascending ser-orpenntis...
Same ancient lineage issuing Ea-Enki-Cyclical Bull.

Would take and Marye to Herself
The Ox-eyed Tanus King was Egypt's Amen-Hophis III,
Scion of The House of Royal Forum In-Karn-Ak-at.
To prepare and thence reveal him latest opus,
Her Aperio Ap Apis.

Tanus taught to be consistent,
To live and serve ' In Truth ';
As king to reign benevolent,
Dispensing nurture all his earth...
His husbandry continuing in the way of Tammuz,
And dedicate to Adonis.

King and God-Queen ruling Fée-Roe,
They dwelled Luxuros by the Nile in Thebes
She and Iapether was Amon-Ia.
Yet were beset by machination undermined subversive...
Burrowed inexorable, hostilities to policies came Ad-Minna's-Tree...
Jealous only to assume Her power the Anti-Ti conspirators
Formed priestly cabal, Ab D'Aman.

Bruited Thebes again, the hieros D'Amn hieratic,

Mounting mighty Bul-Lex, attribution soi-disant,
And honorific issued heads of birds and brutes consulted teraphim -
Their evolution pinnacling as God the Sacred Falcon Rising,
Instrument was claimed the wrath descending
By Priest-Hoods were The Horrous -
Executing Bull Phaerocious paraphrased His Law, Great God was Horus -
Their destruction vowed, who defied or deified old ritualistic laming
Of any female deity's appointed tanus.

Was accorded further word, the populace -
That king - receiving worship as the Amen,
Was solar-god no more than man -
His composition, common mortal - despite the dynastic cellular magic
Stemmed combinant eugenic: gracious his compliments, La Vie Athon.

Then in peculiar concordance with oracular curse,
Happened Amen-Ophis king, obscurely was to die.
And bereft that husband, did next wed Tiyi dynastic mate
Their son the new Akhenaten.

(Forces Apolar had influenced his conception;
You may recall him....

Manifest the syndrome airs anphrodic, blatant Frölick mal-fremix:
From the pituitary imbalance, resulted thighs were lipo-hermephritic,
And processes mitotic of chromomere development were delayed.
Compounded thence its transmutation,
Was an heir malformed by chromatin excess,
Yet suffered symptoms of opposing paucity equal.)

Despite his vaunting slogan ' He who lives in truth ',
In presence of that progeny descended of The Goddess
(Magda Line from largest planet),
Must **any** *son conduct himself, to so exist ' in truth ',*
Acknowledge and advance Her lawful mandate,
Study Fiat Lux and institute the Matriform...
Be he royal born or otherwise.

Shining-Sun-and-Moon ill-starred....
Sullen the muttering in the temple....

Yet not for royal incest were anathematized,
Jocastiyi Couween, and son Akhn-Oedipul Pharonoid Phanatizeal...
Targeted militent search out! then destroy them!
Peace-May-Kuh goddess and abnormal Her kin.

A daughter incarnate the goddess,
Was reason would more than suffice.

(*Scrutiny misdirected oh so cunning!*
As Maide to seem belonged to House the Thebes Atreidæ,
That infamy referred to as tale of Oedipus Wrex.
And problem thus was sidestepped of what was Mother-Son Religion,
Where a son perhaps so treacherous will usurp or murder Her,
Coveting role and function, Her seat of secular power.
Does legend have it did Jocasta hang herself....
{ *Unlike my daughter adrift in dreams,*
Who reprieved, did someway skirt it. })

Remember again the Dove-Soul who bore you:
Created coup Her world...
Sounded coo Her word.
You knew Her, Lady of The Spiral Sound Tree:
Slow opalling waive Her downy wings could raise the sonar thunder clap.

(*Remember her, Io, entrapped the sad lowing,*
Broadcasting groans creatured-vaiche sound,
Kuh bellowed modular mouth:

Yet singing still! the Merer primal magic,
Stringing lexicalpha betomega, life Her dendron trees.

Fording perforce and bhosphorescing,
Creams and churns lakes, Minna-Io, Cow-horned...
Lugeo lachry mot were tears Her only word.)

So they did shun it, Thebes.
Did that city quit forever
Tiyi with Acc-Khey-Naton and supposed their descendant kin.
(Androgynous all, with primary shape like that of women,
Their Worrships, the born-agains.)

Betook themselves downriver,
Erecting there a capital set wondrous jewel the middle world,
Shining Khun-Nu City of The Son...
Consecrate and dedicate God-city, named it Akhet-Aten,

Confirming himself, Akhn-Aten,
New deputy of the first begotten Son of Suns,
He completed for the god an humble temple
Offering become the earthly home his own.

Mighty he strove its construction...
Passing honey days therein,
Writing ode and tribute extolling the celestial god was Aten.

Seventeen years... his ' living in truth ',
Indulged the sweet shelter of Goddess His Wife.

Yet pharaoh was flawed and treacherous, Akhnaton Royal Egypt.
For loyalties acknowledged stollen, was discarded femmilial bonding,
Usurped was precept monotheistic, religion stolen from The Mother...
Whose indulgence led to hubris rotted overweening,
Would to crypt and topple bring them down
Those Oedipul siblings, sons and daughters were their own...
Howsoever was The-Bes-tial brother to them all.

W-Rex again Their Heighnous story!
Boeufari fetialis hits their ostrich fan!
Pried Priesthood fateful foe-tor
Into Codex-Io's propounded evolution...
Malfeasant used its arcane secrets
As but means to prove were not!
Evolved her-storied devilutions...

Then underwrote insidious,
Insurrection infemmous and final!
Reintroducing undercloaca prophecy
Clandestine foretold King Laius' merder
(Accorded with that mystery surrounded father Amenhotep's death),
Circulated after that came Protocols accusing him of patricide,
Unpopular son was Oedi-Pusillanomy.

Implementing next their knowledge gained R. Cane,
The sorrow learned A. Bell -
Infoenis murderers brought them down!
Savaged them fatal the Maide! Her Son!
Corpses disposed ignominious.
(Ay-ling Uncle to Her children was kinsman false, Her Brother Ay.
Ayding ghouls corrupt and blasphemous: priests The Horuscane of Wose.
Ravened after power Mal Ankhanaille,
An abusing sibling yet another one.

Fomenting civic brouhas scanned panoptic: omnispeye its focus,
Covert spied like Argos on its inner life, the palace now unveiled....
Royally removed and unaware the family: Dites-Emvowel! Axed!)

Desecrate and execrate, Her ancient tongue was Coptic.
She who **was** *the Coptis!*
Maide anathema dis-astraed! Defaced. Obliteraced!
Concealed a burial site gouged blasphemous
Where gorged and sank the stinking vulture,
Where slunk the carrion fed.
Tossed as common victim evil plague o'er potters' field of Quebto,
Quen tabooed and lost from sight. Silent Maide the Kupht.

Hauled as rubbled rock, the gloried temple. Mere excavation fill...
Bed foundation supplied his dwelling, the Oediphicial successor.

(Found Min-Isis on that same accursed jackals' field
His sacred corpse dismembered,
Temple housed God-brother was Her Beloved Osiris.
Equal struck the tumbling! reason Maide annihilate!
But would all the same, endure! The Royal The-bes Equepto.
Descendants of House Epaphus and of Io.)

And who assumed their next control, the fabled gold mines?
Three centuries hence same golden ore-acle and liberated ore-phield

Will supply, maintain the wealth and military might possessed by Solomon,
King was foremost of The House of David, his wisdom grown proverbial.

Seyt-âne, Shaitan, Set-Tanus ass head proverbaal,
Set the proverbs proved too many!
He ended reading Baalad ready goaled
Who followed donna key was D'Ora edomite...
Or perhaps was aegyptus Holy Cow....
So long as she Maide gold and did supply it...
What difference?)

Undeniable the truth!
Was overindulged the consort, royal offspring...
Lifelong lacked restraint... waxed predator purveyor of religion
So innovative conceived, would replace them, pluralistic gods...
Endorse the worship Mono-Theo was patently his own and glorified self.

Policy promoted internecine strife
Within his sacrilegious hierarchies...
Shock-troops reinventing gods d'amployed the masses
Devised new canon taking arms against the living;
While polemics mouthed combative doctrine, did but propagandize them.

Inscribed mud-clay were protocols non-sanctitus.
Maide Vehicle Her Word
Directive of the Anti-Path. The Anti-Life.

Never occurs to Her, his mother;
May mistakes overlooked prove but fatal.

As children so many are spoiled and given their way,
Of him, might nothing be asked.
Sufficient Her pleasure might She worshipful serve.

Yet She who was truth and the dweller therein:
Adoring must needs be adored!

Appropriate toward the gods is the quality of deference;
A tribute hardly decent when tendered the unevolved kinder.

(And more gods move earth and heaven
My dear Hilario,
Than might human kind conceive!

Are all of them but I.)

(Once you met young Horus in my dream estate...

Hawk's head derivation enabling without friction,
The fluid slipstream ornisleek...
Flight unencumbered silent, to hurtle silken feathered gloisseau
Interchanged the air....
Oh. Human more than You! Iridescent sculptures fashioned avis kin...

Contemplation of comparison, induced abashment shaming...
Humbled you, Purity stood simple gleaming;
Held you mouton-dumb The Majesty perceived.
Mayhap you dreamed it solar bird that prayed its metamorphosis
Had become the conscious godling...

Beauty was so stunning... withal so fond, so mild,
Scarce could you comprehend at first had issued being new the ranks
Some spirit-flesh or soul was not familiar....

Yet Fellows, both of you within the order's college;
A student was but junior-most... even such as he...
Attainments far surpassing sowing-skein of replicated housings
Contained nobilities the Hu-man souls, did schematic leech, Apollo.

He turned and looked upon you kindly as some shepherd
Fond his dog and lambas husbandry....
Oh. So far beyond you.)

The centuries these... preceded Moses.

BOOK THIRTEEN

NOAH AND HIS SONS

And there were giants... and they begat....
Lived long.

Many are the generations of begatting,
Descendant sons, R. Cain agnomination.
Ultimate condemned ignominate,
And drowned by flood,
Before their god Agnoahstic generations
Grown corrupt is told us -
Peopling violent his earth.

Drowned them then in Heifa,
City of Our Lady of Carmel.
And none but sons of gnostic Noah/Asia was saved atop Mt. Ara Rat
(Become the first was last, new patriarkus Son of Fratricain):
Sons were Shem and Japheth, Ham the youngest.

Directed Jahweh, Thunderer,
' Go phor wood and build your ark,
There mount within it husbandry,
Two of every living creature.... '
But then, you know the story.

Accorded their instruction,
Duly constructed was the Arkus by Noah and his issue,
Who would ride the floods lone arkonauts world-surviving.

Directive once again, their mentor Jahweh
As had once before indoctrinated Adam:
' *Be fruitful. Multiply. Go. Replenish the earth.*
And now may you eat of meat. '
Albeit drowned by flood that earth -
Vanished on it - men and kine.

Sought cleansing of his race their wrathful deity,
Operation could be claimed but small success;
For not yet had lost its savor, A-pellicio sodium-salt,
Odium unsubdued... and sodomy continuing. Worse.
What means **ham** *but hock of beast is cloven footed,*
Perverted man reverted animal satanic, salax the sow-ing unclean?

But accepted were the offerings sacrificial made by Noah to his Iaoh.
Then departing, Shem and Japhaith, did thereafter dwell together.
The destiny Ham's was founding Father of Hus and Land Canaan
(*Country called after that son of Adam, murderer was Cain*).

It is rumored of Ab Gnoah, Patri-Arkus father -
Bacchic in his vinecups -
Exposing naked shame his thigh full view of Ham the second born,
Did drunken curse that son:
" *Shalt be thou chastised! Made servant of your brother! Japho!*
To you is left nought else but life-enslavement
And the single pair of slippers!"

But ' nakedness ' seen the Father's?
Rather was so eu-femmized, the state unmanned and eunuchized
To fulminate oracular like to prophecies came the Arkus.

(*Is told the tale how equally was undone*
By attachment dogged to house and slippers,
A certain rich man, call him Abugh Kasim.
Not to mention soft shod hauslich hunter quarry,
Trod sodalitas the slipper-y,
Sodultima Fule Hussein...
Secret sodalicious hoped to leach the world its oily caverns lucrous,
Contrived its recurrence the rising flood...
Deluge this time... Set shaitanus spill of oil.)

Neither calumnious nor libellous:
Paragraph next cites historical fact.

(*Practitioner of the rites were Dionysian.*
Was by Apollo, Ladan Maide a sadomist,
Though still to father line of Cain slew Abel eaten by the earth...
Phagotrous flesh was swallowed Sarkos-Phagos.
Indoctrinated ritually in partaking of the sperm,
Generations coming after were born addicted to the murderous,
Can-abals lusting the taste of flesh.

Engendered thence was lesbiality and sodmoronis, sterosophity,
Women being instructed similar in the same spermaphagy,
And any other animality inimical to furtherance of the race:
Mortal viciousness late-sprouting, seed was aquernos
Born of Oak was El { De Luge, our Ladan }
Fostered thence by Apollo,
Deadly twin of Lady Maide The Garland Sound,
Our Vox Diana-Lune-Luciphorous....)

For possession of Jerusalem are warring yet, Yehudi,
Desirous of the Hebron Cave Machpelah,

Where was rested Adam, was Abraham enshrined -
Petriarkus fathered all his dispofissioned race.

Not all of them believers from the first, or followers of Jahweh....
Including issue Ben Jamin and Iosephus who faithful worshipped still
The goddess hight Astarte-Hathor, Luce-Venus the Diana...
Preferring not that one did style himself ' Ia-Hu '
God eternal burning lust of for and after,
Sighd-on sighs-fer Code Illustrious -
Arka-Kasha starborn is lost DNA.

Yet for its gain, that sacred Gnoacrostic,
Murderous sacks again the Ham Shem Husse-Incanaan!

Circling annals Maison Meny Peinus that same future,
Sown royal Huss the locus poenitentiæ,
Trapped Fort Domus Lamentari, Lookout! overlook and Belvedere...
Young seeker aging after truth Her Mother
Will think to find Her clan Bi-Lily supern-astral,
Through horos-scryer of astounding name was Lilian Jacques Canaan!
But already progammed in Her brainpan, the tapes named that Shemantic!
While infinite möbius print-outs tickered-hiercowa tripped her own.

BOOK FOURTEEN

THEN WAS JUDAH

Let us consider the tribe Yehudi:
Deriving from it the name of ' Jew ':
S'appelobaum Judahite descendent tree of Judah,
Son was fourth and heir of Jacob who was Israel,
Worshipped god was Yahweh and carrier historical
Of ' The Blessing ':
Berakha same was first received
By Abram from his god.
Be read the oracles.

From Ur was carried into to Canaan,
Abram's father, bore the name of Terah.
Put ahead indeed, this terahscrying tribe,
Filah buried Cave Mach-pelah.

The sacrifice fought Abram with Pan-ic pant ecstatic terrah
Did to Iaohw offer life of son first-born
And thereby save the life I-saak-rifeiste and won!
That god ennobled appelling him next, the new Ab Rah Ham,
One had overcome his primal fear of ram his thicket...
Or indicating alternate, ' The One: The L'Adan Born Again '.
(*Ab-ram means to strive against the natural man of lower mind adamic.*

It is told was Man The Adam born edenic shrine of Heiphron.)

Originally had signified, the willingness blood sacrifice -
No more than psychic symbol.
Yet would soon become the literally performed obeisance
Before omnipotence is worshipped: god inimical without mercy.

Woe the Kow-tow such! Not my particular cup of devo-tea.

(Loomed its shadow panic Butt U-Ram, remember?
But You! who died! Little Ewe Lamb!
And Hephron lived again as vault of death held Heifern was my own.
Vernal springtime heifer on he-broneous,
How knew young dreaming Io of fate receiving death from Goat God Pan,
Same A-b-Ram mocking Holiness revered as brahmin's cow
And egg of goddess B-Rahm-A?)

Wife first espoused of Jacob, kin was his was Leah
(Her name connotes ' The Cow-eyed ')...
Who although did bear him sons
(Of whom above aforesaid... fourth was Judah),
Abode ' unloved ' of Jacob and was not worshipped.

Took him also, Jacob, for his wife thereafter,
Leah's younger sister was Raquel.
(*Progeny both of that uncle, astrologer who was Laban,*
Brother to Rebekah, Jacob's mother).

Raquel sly did carry with her,
Household teraphadim stolen from their father,
He who worshipped it eternal font of wisdom,
Dispenser of prosperity:
Stole it heartless from his dwelling lain northwards from Jerusalem.
Raquel! Child was flesh and blood of Abraham -
Obedient Their Patriarch!

(*Is railing yet eternal scorn,*
All time and future Cundrie. Hah!
Pierced grief the pegs and stakes in palace hearts
As learned what signalled Parzival's lack.)

And all do translate cognomen, variation yet the same,
Is Zhacqe-cub, Izaac, Iaccuh, Yiaco, Dago, Jack and Djiego.
Indicates significance, each rolling scale of Draco,
Merely **Jacques is James.**

(Hired the lawyer's costly jargon,
Legalese interpreted involute the law...
So thankful for prescription rendered scrawled obscure
By specialist leech pretending to Latin:
They do excel! The babblucres your professionals!

Who seeks their advice is confounded...
By the language is cryptic,
Designed to deceive and to rule;
Daily Maide new formulae,
Double-speak grows ever less precise
While spits and screams its dialectics in alienated tongs -
Propounding one and all the war implicit.

So here introduced is the tongue yet another.
Thing to differ this one,
Instructs new way of comprehending sound:
Brings understanding nearer early speech of childhood is forgotten
Issues language-systems sacred nexus
Connected-linkage, human body.
Exists no more than that, the secret,
Yet a truth progressively fugitive.)

Twice we are told did Jacob wed amongst his mother's kin:

Followed Leah, her sister was Rach-El:
Yet early Meccan surahs make the differing claim...
Rather than was son to Isaac, was Jacob really brother.
Jacob. Isaac. Either case,
Most likely one and same,
But continuing thence through time
The tribe was known Is-Ra-El.

Yet should be Jacob simply Isaac,
And both were but personage the same;
Then had Isaac/Jacob married niece
Or grand-niece was Re Beccas:
Those grand-nieces being two,
The daughters of Laban, who was Re Beccas brother.
Eclipsing natural filial love for mother,
The beauteous Rebecca/Rachel was adored.

Hikate Hecate!
Pleasing also to the Single Eye of Ra,
Was earlier appointed concubine and paramour of Pharoah Egypt,

A comeliness favored not easily ignored.
Still... compared but Mère iota
With the moonpearl lustrous was Io.

(*You may have noted somewhere, sometime;*
To save the life his own...

As to his wife-cum-aunt,
Sly had Isaac-Jacob told that Pharoah,
' *The woman is my sister '....)*

And thing should be reminded:
Now carried dual seed her womb, Rebacha;
Bore the nations two!
One, the first and eldest, twin was Esau;
Red Man Hairy Cad Man, hunter of the forest
And by his aging father Isaac, doted on.

Then twining sinuous coming after,
Supplanting all prophetic,
Would gain this elder brother's birthright,
His wily twin the other...

Wrestling precedence in the womb,
Hand clasped about his brother's heel,
Issued comely, Equepto son so smooth of skin,
Second geminus was Jacob.

And Rebachus who was perhaps his mother/mate,
Did this one love the best:
Descendant holy blood occult The Royal House of Egypt....

Userpent issued twinned of sprouted seed secundus,
Was rogue-gene ancient bred...
Strain uraeus iacoh driego
Strayed viaccus cryptric line Maide L'Eg'ypt: Gau Equepto.

(Was promised him the breeding -
Generations hence -
Of that prominence, tribe was Judah
To scatter seed its world like stranded sands the stars;
A diaspora in some future to soar the reach beyond.)

Yet preferred at first the second son,
A simple shepherd life and chambered tabernaculum.

And Esau, cunning hunter,
Loved him well that twin his younger brother...
Not least for benefice of potage,
Venison obtained the forest.
And also could provide it Jacob,
The grain of earth turned into bread...
Cook the bean ancestral lentile,
Stew and spice it hearty soup.

Limping weary from the hunt one day and fit to die,
Did Esau beg from Jacob the provender his pan.

Came rejoinder prompt from canny twin and brother.
' Sell me this day thy birthright. '

Esau answers, ' Look you!
At the point of death what profit me my birthright? '

' So swear to me! ' Demands that Jacob, son of Israel,
And so swearing, Esau did receive the message potage Jacob sold him.

Despised him thus!

That birthright blessed and was his own.
Sold for mess of potage, field Ark-ad:
Dismissing them all as allegory a légume,
Red bean descendants Edomite,
Reborn the spirits ancestral.

Shall all history thus repeat,
Reveal result its purchase and exchange:
The rock. The dome.

She who once was Sarah;
The wife described as sister... call her now Sarai.

Thought signified reborn?
Tradition furthered of the gods?
Her espousement - matriarchal parent taken unto wife?
And Abram, husband fathered many nations,
His name new-given, Abraham.

As Jacob also underwent such transposition...
Would all henceforward know him ' Israel '.

His nomenclature modified same way Egypt,

Amenhotep King is Fourth,
Assuming his new title, Pharoah The Akhenaton.

Even pretender Apollo was desirous of worship as Amen Ray of Light,
Sun-God arcs the traffic spins his world,
Crosses meridian solar trace...
Yet another proclaiming himself the Amen,
The One who was worshipped monotheist.

Whereas do generations appear to skip historic beat...
The truth is they do not.
And if the summaries these stories seem symbolloxed

They come down to you through legend
Reiterate in the western bible.
And much as they read above.

Taking up the authorized, the royal Jamesian version:
One traces obfuscated intertwinings
Of the filial threads and strands tracked back and forth
Its coastal shores and sands the shifting desert -
Crescent riven cradle mid-terrene is deemed The Holy Land.

BOOK FIFTEEN

THEN WAS JOSEPH, SON OF ISRAEL

Celebrated yet, the dreamer who was Joseph:
Son doted on by Israel,
Beloved child of his old age,
Sired last one was known to Rachel:
Her soul departing as brought him birth,
The Ben Iamine.
(Perhaps in some way turned the revenant,
Viaccus strain was issued ancient Egypt.)

Kind of heart was Ioseph,
Never had he wept but was grief for plight another's.
Inherited full the magic genes descended Io
He lived as gifted seer,
Proving true his prophecies and accompanied by wisdom sage,
Avoiding those calamities foreseen the dream-told lain in future,
Howsoever such intelligence be deemed the privy.

For all such magics these
Did father love great soul and mind possessed of Jo-Seph.

But rising jealous, his brothers,
Not least for fair thing wrought him by their father,

A splendid coat was woven rainbow colors,
Betokening very pinnacle the paternus favor.

As envies fraternal were further fanned by younger sibling's dreamings -
Prophecies thought threatened future degradation at his hands -
Then did elder brothers plot against him, conspiring how to slay him;
Until seen lay greater wisdom in selling him slave unto Egypt.

Hoped thereby each one to rid the household
All damned threat and onus: Joseph's Dreamings.

They took the gorgeous coat and rent it.
Killed a goat-kid, smeared and dipped its blood,
His formerly magnificent, now bedraggled garment.

Borne it back to Israel was their father,
Hypocris wept mourning, mummed the diphdhong phoney:
'Look you now, what thing we have found!
Be it this thy son's coat do you know?'

How they viewed the grief their father's
The bible does not say.

Yet Jacob who was Israel
Did rend those garments were his own...
Forswearing all but sackcloth as girt was fit his loins.

But not come sionara yet!
And destiny still protecting,
Does good fortune follow after him,
He who fathered, then was led
By Joseph star-favored, his son.

Stars creating Joseph favorite of the Royal Egypt.
(Do I recall that monarch current was monotheist Manik-henaton?)

Bound the beginning by conventions of enslavement,
He found within those confines the semblance of equality,
Indulgences obtained him audience within the royal palace.
Thus heeded,
Were deciphered dreams prophetic delivering pharanoic warning.
And focused lens his astral sojourns...
Garlands distilling wisdom plucked...
He rendered divination subtle more than kings...
Great The Luminati accessing cryptic image.

Il-luni-mations of their own,
By the fleshpots their hands to offer him interference,
Accursed bacchurs... the Boeutlers of the court.

Yet did rise the star of Joseph over Egypt and there was he secure.
Earning honor waxing ever greater
To grace the fullness of his years.

He it was - fond trickery -
Brought Israel father, all his tribe, to dwell in fertile Egypt,
Settled them amidst the golden wealth of Goshen,
Where they did multiply, become abundant,
Grow powerful in the land.

Then scroll of life completed, Isaac-Jacob's,
Was it yielded up, his ghost.
And carried all his sons the patriarchal corpus,
Returned it to the Land of Canaan...
Where was Israel to his fathers gathered...

And felicitous enfolded within that sacred ground,
He reposed The Cave Machpelah.

BOOK SIXTEEN

EXODUS THE MAGUS, MOSES

As hoved the miraculous once before...
Sailed a Second Ark toward new berth the future...
Attaining final rest amidst the covering reed of flagplant.

Was by Egypt to be harbored,
The infant, Moses,
Floated hostage tiny ark his waters,
Converging destiny Arkane at last
Would lay him safe enfoldment of her arms,
The Lady who was Miriam: Daughter of Great Egypt,
Princess known for wisdom, royal favorite of that house.

(*Comes variation yet another:*
Of legend claims im-acca-lait the boasted birth....)

Those there are make claim that Miriam was his mother.
So partially at least,
Would the blood of Moses be Egyption.
Howsobeit, he was raised Equiptos Prince high and royal,
Adept attained to high degree and a fully accomplished magus.
Whether prodigy was Jewish, or initiate of Egypt unacknowledged,
Did no one dwell that land might say him nay.

And yet... and yet...
Despite instruction in deep magic,
By misfortune or design,
Perforce would Moses seized the stutter mouth,
Exile himself forever from that haven Egypt,
Host had shown him kindness:

Came the fateful day, his wrath aroused,
He did slay a man was native to that country.

Across the years had come these later generations,
Pharoahs ruling who knew not Joseph,
Their former guardian of prosperity.
Fearing now might land be taken from them,
They considered how to rid themselves of those so many...
Too powerful. Too rich.

' *Lest they make treaty with our enemies*
And take arms against us...
Escaping, leave the country undefended...
Wherefore let us now enslave them. Wear them down.
For never shall I let them go. '

Overseen and heavy loaded,
The Israelite was put to labor in the fields;
Turn clay to brick then haul it,
Install and build new cities.

So oppressed, he yet did multiply.

Issued therefore edict new, the Pharos:
' Remove each boy-child born to them.
Cast it thence the river! '

Revenge fell swift.
Yet before consented Pharo next to free them,
He would suffer the jewish god's nine plagues -
Plus delivery of their death-strike
All first born of kin and kine
That dwelt in the Land of Egypt.

In terror of assault come further at the hands of unrelenting Iahweh,
Egyptians then themselves elected their own plunder,
Pressing prodigal on former slaves all personal gold and silver ornament,
Should these but speed the Israelites' departure.

Some years pursuant his adventures,
Was Moses sojourned in the land Medean.
Came upon him - not to be denied -
Intelligence was celestial,
Annunciation from within the burning bush
Was bush which did not burn.

Lifted up, he did exhort him, Jahweh.
Nay directed...
Had gained that mastery over Egypt's magic:
Now must he **use!** *its might.*
Set free from persecution!
His people groaned on genocide.

Many and compelling were his arguments
Should Moses lead their exodus,
Guide those tribes of Israel,
To that country promised was Canaan.

Followed therefore hence the Israelite and Hebrew faithful unto Iaoweh,
Followed overlord was Moses
Who took them out of Egypt -

Unto this day recounted
Is the fearsomeness endured those toilsome years
Seemed lost migration aimless -
A waivering surge but thither and yon
The crossing inimical sands:
Their flight in horror before it,
Illimitable host was Egypt...

Vowed, despite the known persuasions and influence was Iahweh's,
To reduce them back again to slavery, all their tribe!
For mighty vexed was Pharoah as learned Young Moses
Did abscond with Magic Rod, The Living Language Tree:
Treasure meant to reproduce its vivication, Dynasty!
Stole them! birthright formulæ genetic
Shapers of Betraides, Io's line:
Cow-ferry plunging long ago, world-cirkuts,
Io heifer, frantic fled Accadia.

There was more:
By Jahweh fed the Holy Mannas Substance!
White showered from the sky,
Had nourished them those straggling hordes,

Some of whom remembered Egypt and were grateful.

(But infant memory formed too young
Retains recall refreshed by nothing! lain beyond
The wilderness and savage.)

Notwithstanding, people of the exodus
Did reinstate the Imag-Ka, The Esoter Ad'Aurum:
Rendered her, Io, Loose-Heifer The Glowing Kalf,
Carved her Exo-tera from castings formed rough gold.

Gorge waxed hot at pagan warship,
Old testor mentor cursed them flat!
Spewed execration at their love for Gau,
For joy of man's desiring - peace and simple.

Then next did smash those covenants, Moses,
Hard fetched from the mountain,
Tabula etched in stone.

For who now sang homage heathen god,
He proposed the punishment! ***hommerde!***

(Although not totally expunged were the devotees these.)

Myriad his titles,
But there existed only one adversary promoted the Bi-accus;
Legerdemain alone produced the pantheon self-designate,
Jahweh, Iahu, Zeus, Apollo et al..
Yes. Always Your Lady's age-old twin and heinous brother.

(Let it now be said:
Not I had Maide him, Chrisos, aped the crescent-horn Ac Apex!
Who worshipped golden bullion his,
But served his own undoing!

Mentioned has been sometime Maide
How gods did cherish the element gold:
Component activates longevity - the life perhaps aethurnal -
Or - conflated tally, bior-lectron part am-ore-tal.
Could not be common greed for gold!

Else might worship Jacqual Typhon Set his asses ears!
Human voice balaame, or she-ass ânah,
Oracle d'or'is c'unabula!)

Moses, gorge waxed fiery hot again,
To the furnace ordered melt-down all ornaments and idols.
Chastised them faithless irreverdoters his errant people,
' Such love have you for gold! Shall you therefore eat it! '

Apolleyed the law, force-fed them: engorged them liquid gold!

Subdued, the D'oras!
By separating healthy cell rad iotard re-iostope
Induced convulsion epileptoid,
Radical colloidal rampaging rad'auru'm.
Maide of them the governance Mosaic,
Were asses Midass-es ill indeed!

Gold was needed, yes...
But more as served accomplishment of subtle circuitry
Beyond his ken or capability...
He who erstwhile had honored and revered magicianship.

Was the latter day Wilhelm Reich ensanet of this.
Progressively prognostic,
Speculated spirit-gold was disappeared,

Equating the lack with anti-life-d'or!..
Fought un-adoring bio-rebel cell, first toiled and sought to add-ore.

So how should be maintained,
Let alone replenished, aggregate the ore?
How obtain keye psi-cells living,
Convert the mortal flesh to everlasting raiment d'or?

Fond Goddess did promise them this!
Could magic hers deliver anything!

But already was inculcate and fundament of faith -
The love of D'Oro Gold.
Manipulated atavistic behavioristic base,
He was ensured of gold production,
The Apol D'Ore Yehahoo.
Business his? ***Oh. His business was religion!***
In gold may it trust.

Receiving neither gold nor benefice a peaceful age,
Prophited in nothing, Moses,
Vision deuterrabil, sinaicus aganostic of the magus:

Except perhaps his view of Luck Out!
Sight the promised land wherein he might not enter.

Man waxed full his years and height his powers,
And of future there was none!
Cut down the days were his at Moab overlooked the plains.

Delivered us next the centuries,
Yehudi kings the first were Saul, then David.
(*Youth would slay the Philistines' Gau-liath,*
Giant sent against him.
{ *Did landed sons of Stone and Holy Pælex,*
The Dagon Mermaide worship:
Possessed and knew it natives for Her region,
Land of Phalœ-stine }).

BOOK SEVENTEEN

THEN WAS SOLOMON

Culminating Patri-king and Trois-Ark,
Furthest flower was Solomon...

Sang canticles his songs of love and wisdom -
Lain their embraces, the mana-foaled affections
Of his many and varied mille-fleur wives -
Magus greatest favored by the goddess -
Distillator of the law.

Unburdened by god-fealty growing, served Jahweh,
Yet was he become proverbially rich
Beyond all dream of avarice...
Exacting from his twelve and factioned Hebrew tribes
Their golden talents every year -
Ever amounted in mystical tally to number was ' 666 '....

He was to navigate the straits Ore Muse,
Discover Solomines the Ophir gold....
Gold was hewn as stone in measured cubit
That fit the temple Hiram built him.

Came gold of value even more from Jouffre

(Dweller as the genie of En-Gulphment, El L'Adan,
Djinn-Keeper of that famous treasure
Deep cached its vaulted caverna);
Ancient Codex, Tables Secret Ori-Genal,
Golden Science vocalized the Dorac Oraclef.

Pondered it.
Ingested its instruction -
The orto-guardened ophis godhead.

Enlightening him the message potent poetage Diennae,
Grammar spelled filaine the primal thread -
He attained to lux did wrest redaction of that wisdom
Buried under fallen tower lay rubbled Babyl Chowos:
And in harmonic chant of orison new polished,
He breathed new life revivified the ancient langs
Voiced long ago by drifted poets arisen ancient heart-worlds.

Then calm awaited Wizdomed Genomene immort,
The Orphanes pearl his great descendant.
Magus abiding, parse-ceipheral tells it,
In tenuous and extended temporality -

Until was manned again, Ark Solomon's,
Vessel royal plunged the seas, Third Escort bound its mission -
To enfold him, dispatch his safe arrival to ancestral bosoms,
The chivalrous and faithful Galahad.

(*Though some do claim true distant heir solemnic,*

Had borne first naming L'Ancelot: whence baptized anew,
Had duly established his sacrifice of ' natural man ',
To become the Brightish and transcendent Gau-Lahdan { Galahad }).

BOOK EIGHTEEN

JOSEPH THE ARIMATHEAN

Parsed it oporstutas!
Iusoph Arithmedea Fissureman the First,
To de-clarify misleading:
Seph Medea is the message!

Kuhndig of coven,
Likening himself in part
To salmonon konig old testraumun
Conversant with the alloguence existential
Keyed nucleus forming family and the child,
He sees to it are spirits sacret borne beyond the med-seas:
And there will hunt them down like rabbits,

Will bring to ground such upstart
Was ever proclaimed new messiaghe.

Carried them Josuph
To Britain
As hound that ran with the heires
Were the legatees of life cells -
Root and branch the tree devine.
Held them fast the exile of that distant northern home.

Protector was trusted.
Persuading them provided haven safe
Where they might reach no harm,
Sequestered and established far from roth of split-off faction,
Discib-lingus the Petrus rock...

Again conspiring propadanga cruciphal,
The encyclical issued Roman bull:
More than testament new mess age,
Pronounced it miranchorl infallible,
The event at Geth-seman Boulder:

Christ victorious over death arisen!
Resurrected, lives again!

Deep the Deltio'd fissure,
Domiciled existence alongside papal rule!

Was meanwhile fishouse mathia, too ambitious
For attainment any sainthood!
His reward appropriate and prompt
Came deservèd testa-maiming!

Yet occurse! his ongoing privilege:
Contender schemes for hierecular crown served secular,
For mitered cap proclaimed him holy.

Diseased exploiter of the Grail Power
Flourished on malfeasance - that self-styled Fisharking.
Was like Anfortas and the wizard Cling-sor,
A lecher avarishi and automata alchatamite...
Money changer ever ready before the sore and time worn Alter,
Clings-ore metal.

By jailer of the Dias Missal gaelic mythic legend,
Was swallowed up true history of the Grail:
No guardian of tradition,
But warden burying Her his keep,
Columbe and the infants Her kinder,
Holding them hostages ransomed,
The Fisher-Skeine.
Pirated were rosters and tables the summaries her works,
Geneal columned Her pristine kin...
Registers plagiarised these...
Contrary set to rank purpose confounded their own.

Oh. They would bring the world down!
Only helped them rule.
If not the mineral klinkers planet,
Then at least destroy organic life upon it,
Sailed wing or fin, or trod by foot.

Is sabotaged each single life -
Gathered up all residue of seed first Maide,
With patternings of intention rewritten subtle and debased.
And earth first learns of poison, absorbing bloodshed and death.

Be-acchursed apauline pollo!
For maimed and fissured spawnings his.
(*Nought else but egg-and-dart comprises Goddess Line.*)
He has sought to rid the world of influence is mine.
Cur-tailed, encrypted, the holy blood goes underground,
Except as did subsist at fairy court of venulot.

Xatholixed was every isle of greater brightain.
Vitiate and subverted, the early celtix churches....
Is by Roem-anxhs absorbed my every name.
Sacred nouns were Marrye Verghian Mother,

Conveyed but Mere conjugal! The accessory reduced.
By papery fallasyllabius Maide servant to wholly roman censure
That incessted was The Magdalen
Maryied to the young son god was crucified,
Chrystos mystos resurrected from the coils of death....

Did rise the Grail from line of Iudah is claim untrue.
Were tables peopling eden overturned by fisharks anamathea!

Brideags to pronounce them, heathen heresy bred low breugash!
A waste of time the academic quibble: Mab in Ogam Sanctus!

So much for eloquence,
Its promised love and testameant
New Head above the old...
Emphasized the missales battle cruixer vessel
God-Ship-A-Paulo dogtrine!

Moloch absorbing, swallowed whole
The ritual sacred furthest Thule and celtibration pagan.
As were those truths existing independant doctrine
Adapted clumsy mix of holy blood on platter

Alleged was distillation fresh received
When shed from cross golgothway tree...
And granted to his servant by the lord of hosts and eucharist...
Boon miraculous set him free that Joseph,
Took him from his prison cell death knelly agon penta,
Where lo had languished, bedded sewerpent klinker coals
To plot the centuries of straterage revenge and revenguehes:
Commencing massacres of heretics: pagans forsworn of the cross.

Principle unchanging:
The goddess life is warred against:
And now does Ladye's Oil Her Blood
Burn killer-air, en-gulf the slick.

Knew-clear wins for future,
Lexic nookalert new testorment,
Rabid tort and torcher lusting fire and bortchure,
Rabble overruns and scorches earth:
Ordur born of Worm Ore-Robberuhs

Other times plucks gobbets from the death-plague flesh,

Shot on high from mangonel a rain of mortifying strain Ebola:
To drop opposing armies dead in place
Defending of their towers.

Provides advantage further, proposes death prepared least costly,
And having widest effect: occasioning dementia epidemia
Fears lurking of the virulence on every random surface...
Cringes in avoidance, the visual planes of veriest stone.

Other times, and other flesh...
Comes chaos-germ shot hypodermick,
Death by their hands little heroes, rude hirudos, merdick men
Who will repent their agon in the future,
Affect concilishun as world troops unite new coilickum.

Suffers every attribution Mary's, its spiritual despoilation:
Queen defends our mid-gard Heaven, life is her symbol shown snaked!
Reduced ore-robourous serpent, neither dragon was nor fish...
But messurpent melange, same affinities accorded scorpion's poison.

Until they have faces... shall sons profâne of Aleph Andelph
Be Maide to fear them! Rishis, Potentates An-Cepheathens.

Not of time, The Grail.
Yet manifests within, without...
Encompassing those multiples of dimension
Convention views simplistic as Merely four.

When time is conceived as linear process,
As chrono-logic premised on a ' Now or Then '
It does not address reality
Existing Fundament Unfolding,
Issuing time organo-spatial -
A prospect forever lain vastly beyond...
The Lotus Expanding, Time Everlasting.

Yet cognizance of amplified dimension
Makes unthinkable such proposition might be divided from itself,
Or in any way reduced could function as separate segment of its own.

So bear with me. And vault these seeming incommensurates....
Unaccomplished any victory over mortality,
And programmed those expectancies anticipate of death
That entrap him inside his failing cell.
He lives condemned, the human...

Thus delusion seeming sweet, sustains him,
Girds him phantciful against the life he may not comprehend as One,
Megomanic pitiful, straining ultimate endeavor
Which seeks but tyranny over others.
His hope perhaps - to excel in nukiller psigh-thought
Ticking athombes disconnect and terminal.
The while presumes existence of his own, nonaccountable.
Isolate, Removed.

Is by and large cerebrally tallied, his input of impression;
Due to registers immune to greater systems bi-organum,
He must conjure perforce some partial premise
That genetically can not be sustained.

Follows all report its input, the dissociate human brain,
Follows time-chronostic logic.
Follows Cronus!
Follows sable Father Time, marches on mortality.

Symbolized him Cronus, bears death come sickle or scythe.
Mown them down, voracious eats his children,
Saturnic death, titanic time.

Indulgence of same unbridled appletites ab-famminal
Whereon will gorge Malle Phagos is Apollo.

* * *

Circular thought A Round-Table. Chaotic.
The nonce to intervene, does retaliate The Grail,
Demonstrates invention entered into physic-atom mode ætheric...
Aspect is but differing weight... same thing....

Bested him, the Goddess Life Gen-Viv or Vivinanna,
Bested future Merlin Hawkthought: set his schemes to nought,
Maide him Jacqual Victor Miser.
Yet must she journey still from Karma lot to Caer The Spirit Sorros!
Wayfairing forest satanic Stenay, or bitter tread New Sherwood....
Then stung brocadé,
Flee Brittany from dark les arbres Brocéliande....

Resting at last glorbterra,
Lighted by moon-gild of Lilys the goald...
Reaching Chatone-Nugator En Ogam,
Loqui receiving of schooling came L'Origen à Provnance.

BOOK NINETEEN

CAER GLOSS. THE HOUSE OF GRAIL

Use the gloss. These keys.
Each one accesses cryptic tongue deployed the subtle worlds,
Dynamics resurrecting as new vessels sailed your dreams,
Buoyancies to navigate the oceans of unknowing....

As creator-student of emergent image, name it;
Then roll it dazzling on your brain and give it tongue....

Associating sound that leaps its evocation,
Discover the omni-valence
Developing recombinant in your mind.

Instructed new progressions budding fractal
Soaring catenate, etymographlinks net-worked
Cabled gloss of any dictionary to hand...

Learn the Language Lo-qui is New-Cleyus...
Not merely hyphen-space
To lie between two words policing fore an daft!

Properly read, are meanings multiordinal then perceived,
The signific of word-sound being symbolized thus:

\↕/
<--O-->
/↕\

No time-continuum dream-rumbling on rails, puffing, buffered trainlike.

-->-->

So what in truth do I seek to show?
Traced what thread is held so fast,
Revealing of theft? Debasement? Gyp disguise?

Evolved tradition more than esoteric... secretive, occult...
Touched down on H'earth before was worship risen from Sumeria:
Before was wrought the version neo-human was Apollo's:
Brain-programmed for the ages as digger rooted after gold.

Moch-machines made fila...
Pella skein and thread ancested terror beaming
Smile Lazardus rictus,
Grimoire masked
The tastebuds reached to anus,

Wished bonded only other men... were femmy-men:
Wished births were only made couvade...
New creation of Apollo.
(*Oh! Bananal his repudlick!)*

Complained of language ' Seemed not language ',
' *Cryptic, inaccessible ', or ' exceeding difficult was Maide '....*
Pah! Was the heirarchy hirudo who taught deceit The Word
While played in fields the bawdo....
Those who most! should understand the script of truth -
Plan furthermost its evolution.

Lapsed comatose who can not read me!
Sadyrliarts mooning brain-dead....
Managed even so to drop the bomb atomic!
How now pretend should anyone envision,
Or formulate truth's structure?
Reached on tragedy the Ludwrick!
Yet not poenitet the red phoenicians:
Death-whoring and its penitence
Ascribed instead to Magdalen
Was sistered Marthe and Lazarus.

No. Not going anywhere. Not without the wings.
You have the leathery kine. Then there is feathery kind.

But mean the service now plyed others' ends,
Grail is High, Grail is Holy!
Capable of all things,
Is Filum Mother, Sonar Spiral spelled creation:

With polished lens of rounded crystal focused sonne-light:
Brought it down, as needling light,
And cunning Maide it fire
To quicken flesh was Hers, provide its animation...
Laughing Lady was The Golden Spiral Filum
Winding sounding tree Her Eggrdrasil....

Multiplied here
First magic tail of Hlaffa loaves
And salt sel little fishes
Were cells donated from His Body,
Greatest God His Seas:
La Vie L'Athon The Ever-Renewing
(Our Accsyr or Oxy-rrhynch-us).

Gathers Her crystal divinely its fire
To flash as bolted light spear,
Grêle Hail Maiden, Potter of earth Her clay...
Targets spindle-focus on the mounds
Those formings Her new vessels.

Bright arabesque came light and holy sound
Her voice, instructing DNA
To draco-woeuvre creature-shape,
Combines and enters min-biology prepared,
Weaves cohesion of the filius and the filia....
Dispatching their descent, Maidonor,
New-grown egg and dart ionic,
That solidify in bio-time....

(*The story is told of Prometheus bringing down the sacred fire,*
His liver torn eternal-daily by the beak of eagle sent by whom?
Revenge was wreaked so hellish could none but Apollos devise it.
Promised thus was mankind! Promised by deus! That god forbidding!)

Heavy laden Her tree of life, calices pulsed creation,
Built building block A-starta ashlar: man come full-grown the Ormus.

Then forming you, the Hu Man,
Maide vessel new life was same as Her own,
To attain same destiny... become Eternal Grail
Would bend their light, the spheres...
Refractions showed you heaven,
Bore you pinnacles of consciousness where fulfilled was all desire....

Holy was your consciousness. Your deed.

Fecund was fruit of Tree Sor-Pentine
(Sucred Cells immored La Véda-Ionné, the treasure true).
Yet guards it ill, Lug-Ladan;
Languished heavy somnolence of draco sinué,
Balance is Ladanse askew.

Reputed the eye never sleeping!
Laitin L'Aurum Orme.
Yet was not Maide that first report
The charge of auram fleecing!

Was from Red Cadaman'Deve purloined the golden appol Ore-boeus,
Fruit d'espered the garden Golden Io's.

Maylan famel created She them.
King or peasant...
Do all come down from Ladan.

Mythos misdirecting, relayed throughout all time;
Claims each one originated Genesis:
A thing was never true.

Whom you believe to be The Adam:
He it was, The Ladan
That fathered children of your earth.

Like to the Minerva springing stature fully grown adult,
I Maide him mascul prototype -

Strength never walked the earth as genus giant Gau,
An earlier kined of race.

BOOK TWENTY

JASON, LADAN, AND MEDEA

First bestowed the name of Dio Medes,
It was his tutor Cheiron king of centaurs,
Invested him new Jason.

Before was Son of Jae,
Was father, son of Ae Son,
King of Iolcos
(Sired by Dionysos),
Whose kingdom being overwhelmed by Pelias
(Brother, kin to him),
Did acknowledge that Pelias as the country's next protector.

But was always plagued Pelias that Aeson would quit Iolcus,
Hand Jason to the care of Cheiron,
Saving face the interim
Until such time was Jason reached sufficient age to mount the throne,
Attempt assume its rule, the country rightfully was his own.

Grown tranquil wielding royal power
Encompassing the next decade
Did Pelias act as regent
Disquieted only by that prophecy would sometime danger come to him...

Arriving its guise, a one-sandalled man.
Jason, of such prognostication ignorant, and attaining now to manhood,
Existed compromised by destiny implacable ordained,
And the yoke at first borne dual was become a burden more his own.

Lacked land... political status of any sort...
Hard pressed did Jason follow counsel
Came his friend and mentor Cheiron,
Who, repeating to his protégé
The story of his birth and birthright,
With claim possessed beyond all others',
Sent him on its quest - the fabled Golden Fleece.

(Ventured forth.
Encountering so miraculous the Olympian was Hera,
He was not to note was lost his sandal,
Gaulosh remained in the sand....)

And presenting himself forthwith at Iolcos,
Where he thought to claim his heritage,
By Pelias was he recognised as the stranger long foretold,
The one to come half shod, deliverer of his harm.

Sly embraced his nephew and won the young man over;
Encouraged him avuncular to find the Golden Fleece,
His hope could set to right their wrongs thereby...
Of suffering, ease his people.

By dreams of glory thus inspired,
The thoughts mayhap heroic,
Then manned Jason, vessel of his own, The Argo,
Embarked upon the destiny awaiting him lay Colchis.
Sailed by way of femous Pool Euxinius
(Black Pollute you will remember).
Sworn his service to Athena,
And to that Inarchus, river god who fathered Io.

He would prove however,
The husband wedded more his fate.
And to subsequent betray them,
Demigoddess had become his wife,
Medea... all their children....

(A wisdom so revered by people of her country
They considered her Athena their Goddess had returned.)

By cad lived tainted mortal, by son of Adam Kad man yet half-red,
Was that lady, vessel of his seed forsaken,
As he, enamoured of a younger princess maiden,
Creusa Glaucous, thence took her to himself....
Drove her mad his coma!
Wife wedded to the husband rendered blind.

(*To hang blind cruciform the gallows,*
Augur sufficient persuading the many:
Is preferred the cross christos to grêle.

Are benighted cauldrons still eschewed
As pagan devil-bred... dead revenants reviving,
Arms are borne again, in resurrection.
No cult inquisitorial crusade the crux salvation,
But anathema horrifying even worse: the un-dead sol-dier pagan.)

Look you what befalls him next, the Jason!
Will not edify, his story:
One of faithlessness and wiccard wizard treachery:
Lust and love of gold:
Children blameless murdered vile....

Things occurring long before induced their sleep,
The coilings heavy Laden:
Nought purposed but the senturies as lain in snaked unconscious.

Story tells his end, the Dragon Ladan,
Was for a spell the river God renascent,
Eyes his glinted springs, rising breath his misted streamings.

Should he be revived some distant future,
Will be likely vanished every remnant of his name.
Yet as much as Jason and Medea is this the story his:
Child of Serpent tricked of fleecy gold that hung his tree,
The Golden Tree of Life, its fruit...
Whereon he slept man-dragon sleep psycastrate.

He shall through the millennia be overcome
By killer Sons of J. and Dionysus,
Huntsmen track insatiate, hungering after gold,
By Medea's magic screen bewitching, ensorcelling all.

Mock quest seeks to cross beyond it, River Jordan...
Pilgrimage of some kind to the Holy Land shall ever be...

But to founder soon,
Mad thrall and worship of mercantic mammon,
Plies creusade immerced a commerce
That accursed does buy and sell,
Reduce the wealth of earth
Was Maide the bountied goddess.

Unless accrued by despoilation,
Or by degradation of her riches and immolation of her fruit,
Only then accounted as good fortune was their own:
And guarding which,
Pursued but further massacre and rapine plunder.

Such were these the Cadmeans.

' *Earlier came Canaan (country was fathered of Ham),*
Invading, occupying thence the mountains,
Frontier lain Ionia and Caria;
Conquering next the city, holy Argaus,
Place enshrined the peaceful goddess
Thought sailed bright horned moon her sky:
To sow there dragons' teeth!

Dogtrinal larynx barked new bæhne,
A harm did force the mouth, mis-shaping it,
Corrupting open vowel sound as twisted Syne-alepha.
Adulterating attribution, Vowelle tone was Io's:
That purity unalloyed, sound came the very first,
Maide conveyance of no further meaning is articulate,
Mutated and delivered smeared,
Con-sonant chokes its gutteral stridor,
On teeth clenched rigid the foaming slaver
Psychopanting warfare -
Mongrel rabid blubbers rabble-babble frenzy mongered,
Holds itself superior to Quihotes,
While subscribes in truth to Chaos
Splits on fractalized apartickle
Over and over, and over again....

Down-flings them into second pit of Tartarus,
Confining those are still described, ' the living ':
World is toxic rules the soul,
Where occurs purgation not any,
But is undergone instead the virus rot of braincell,
Inhibitor striking vengeful....

Endless dogmastiqued such brain,
Fever-tuned drumbeat bitten steel-sounds,
Mob-psychoslogged and pounded primeat rage to rabid zealot
Rallied caterwaul Aphilibust unceasing...

Exhausted, is coerced con-sonant vice
By blarings of the great and windy horns trump platitudes,
Blast brainwash of applied semantic new-inverted,
A daily sliding index of shifting truths and honor:

Growls its bully-mutter now,
' *Self-rule to prophet-nation* ';
' *Defy ubiquitous evil even to the death,*
Destroy The Foreign Great Satan and wreaker of sin! '

Had national morality formed religious identity
Was soon repressed by cynical gloss of Parti-pule!
Ja-quelled them: pitiful how easy,
Militent church was the state,
By jingo was pediculous -
By burning slogans did compel.
By the focus of mind fire on critical mass.

Was liberty lost. As often, life.

Caused demediocracy suffering, everyone:
Pressed moment to moment cajolement
Of broadcast black concept was ceaseless revised;
Was bred zealot obsessive to scrying
Led bloody unleashing of Armigidd Threat.

Equipped them always thus!
Armed their jehad: ***Apalaver!***

Search out the keys in this dark tale so needfully abridged:
Slip in and out of lineal time with me.
Absorb these annals as images
Of film swift-shifted sina-mat event,
And your time compress same focus flickered olden measure nephilim;
Should next be traced meticulous the skein strung mazed
And crossed its net and nexus labyrinthus
Wherein was prodigal magic so wanton abused.

Was glared at by envy Apolloptic...
Waxed apocalyptic the planet....

Howsoever was accomplished, vital that you understand
Imperatives of quick and tortuous flight of truth
From trick that left behind but sterile ground hard won,
Bled battlefield of Grail survival.

And wheresoever borne old caelum magics,
Subsequent subverted, were stollen its thieves.

Yet still may soul extend on wing intended:
Cross death-bridge time is catenary bardot...
Avoid the seeming judgement is but rêve of dream.

Condemned. To dream! *There! You have it!*
Exiled living, awaiting dying...
Hostages held by their dreamings of life.

Human arrived new birth,
Is concealed his former death lain hidden inscrutable time.

Yet understood the common usage,
Those flag-starred words of time and space, hold meaning multiordinal,
Compress significance so dense as is only sown confusion;

But it should prove possible to modify the folklore
Makes acceptance of that verbal premise,
Does death bring end to life.

Arrivals many the births. The deaths.
Whereas occurs but once,
That first and single planetary waking.
Yet even death brings welcome sleep
That flows to dream of life again,
Whereby is rebirth promised, attained to the immortal.

Yes. To die. To sleep.
To dream that one is born again...
My dears!
The fight is but to hold the soul against the daily sleeping!
Harbinger certain, foretells of its death.

Pineal is turned the fungal suet,
Fixed amber-graisse its bead brain,
And is left no taste for taste of life....

And denaturing it,

Acquires the preference perverted...
Taste for death!
Creature biped. Quadruped. Omnivore Apolar.

Do not take objection to my timing chrono-sequence:
Do not view my space-time as net is stretched Mere poesy!
But read in there the truth is new-sized,
New-tailored to your understanding.

The histories are all in.
Absorbed and reabsorbed....

And truth so tampered,
Wields influence more than if was buried:
Regalement nothing more than anti-femimystic shauvingays
Wheeled revisionist amd propagandaze
Broadcast wiseards ruling wizendumb.

Allusion cited here so plentiful,
Might well appear too burdensome -
Were realities it describes not so meagre
As to render the world itself allusion.

Not to forget, this history
And what is referenced here:
Pain the most terrible and frightful
Borne by human mind's parabola.

Yet allusion can restore an energy of life,
A thing so real, is overlooked:
Gone unseen: unworshipped:
Is perceived but thing pedestrian.
Or might as quickly hove illumination to astonish!
Albeit did such revelation remain significance unfathomed.

Van Gogh the example:
Painting entity was subtle-body -
Framed god-simple his chair -
Dimension supranatural.
Yet from such as this is drawn the goddess strength:
For lack of which shall you surely die.

This story of the world
Is the story of the goddess' world
And how she would defend it:

Rescue and retrieve it
From progressively stony graveyard,
Inhabited sepulchritude:

From oracles babbled hell's torments,
From oraclef saddled sperm pacts,

From fell and sable shapings legion lain The Shadow,
Name of Darkness Lesion
Cast by brother-twin Dyonesewes,
Ruler Host and Liege dire cancer cell and epidemic plague,
Sorcerer sower of seed the phagos sewercel circle:
Apallo your Diabalow...

From malison called on lightless winter
Lèse-humanity induced new climate cold and spirit freezing,
Left glace moraine
A soil had nurtured flower, The Human Sol.

And seed not any, returned its earth,
Nor spring
Brought forth ongoing life.

BOOK TWENTY-ONE

ARTHUR AND HIS KNIGHTS

Rex Artorius.

By devizes issued sinuous,
Groswhit crest his helmet,
And Her Ikon Shield:
Our Lady Fair was Brigit....

He had yet to live as a man:
Neither crowned her beloved,
The woman his mate;
Nor adept in his knowledge,
The science of love.

And served or known no one ruled greater...
Was reluctant to forswear Our Lady, quite,
Withhold from her its attribution
The rightly famous derring do....

Between two masters torn his Heart.
Expedient,
Invoked those aegises belonged to either.
Sanguine was protection doubled.

But he who harbored hope so base, despised,
Was then upheld by neither!

(*Had pledged himself the Champion Hers.*
Imprinted first by Seal, his flesh,
Lock-set with key was Her own.)

Yet lost to Ancient Crescent!
Ensign emblazoned The Warring Cross
Acquired by marriage to his Queen Guinwoevre:
Damsel The Dancing Christian. (As well be be Dancing Iblis!)
Inevitable should Merlin, pagan, lose through error....

Was servant catholic to Rome, Guinevre...
Its vassal vowed.
Yet decision of the Grail itself, Maide dispersal of their order,
Knights of Arthur, Companions of The Table Round once seated them.

But event too late transpires alas!
Accomplished already the schism initiated mission romish -
Rent and split is kingdom newly wrested from the best came western world,
World was Arthur's, so toilsomely hard forged.

As had heeded Guinevere's persuasion...
Then was Arthur England, lost.
Yes. And with him, all his cycles... Lancelot,
Whose son firstborn was Galahad attained the Grail.

(Lost to his Goddess also, king was Clovis Merovingia...
Badgered too long by his Catholic queen Clothilde,
Rewarded her indulgence by succumbing to religion was inimical.)

Merged them one, the myriad kingdoms first disparate,
Did Arthur new crowned king
Beat down oncoming hordes, implacable expansionists.
To the north and to the south, everywhere he fought ' the heathen ',
' Berserkers fierce and savage, worshippers of Wodin:
Needful some among them of no other god than axe.

Flushed new success unsubsided, tasted state ' heroic ' still,
Would Arthur counsel thoughtful for policy of acceptance and absorption:
' Look you! Are these the bloody soldiers yet so recent?
Well! Colony thrives industrious now! Let us praise the land's subduing
As evidenced by such sober squatters.
Craft to teach us much, this husbandry...

Benefice could heal New Britain... a fruitfulness to make for peace '.

Was brought his country in this manner, sometime pause to prosper.
And should tranquillity prove not the guerdon sought...
Appropriate only then, the question: ' On clay! What ails thee? '

(Still enlightens, Liberty, New World;
Torch aloft on compassion universal,
' Bring us your suffering... your poor ' ...

Are thus the hordes ***invited!*** *from perimeter to pole.*

No less bloody the struggle: expansionist continuum if you will.
Arrivals lately, not simple races one or two,
But swarm proliferate and illegal, self-proclaiming brigands
Give no quarter in the war conducted that is but other kind:
Gang pack-predators gutting colon-eyes,
Knived envy-eyes stabbed hurtful:
' Your money! Smack! And get a life! Get smack! '

Beyond brute expertise purveyor dealing street drugs,
Borne no other talent the avalanching mobs of demoschatic breeding.

And only rarity in fact, the specimen politico, new-termed the refugee.

Oh so chancy beckoned, humanity adrift, a flotsam disenfranchised.
While concealed lie systems apollonian seeking rule:
Accomplished and completed, supersedure...
Will then divide and fracture...
Subjugate by quelling...
Undermine the mass morale.

' *We want your taxes. Want your money.*
Support our fight with crime.
Help us put these roustabouts and indigents away. '

Mostly European strains believe and bear ' The White Man's Burden ',
Are strung on expectation of their law and order.
' *What are taxes for alors? If not provided safety?*
It isn't safe to walk our streets.
Streets are no longer our own! '

Mostly European strains who ousted Indian peoples,
Boasted, took the prize of country. Beggared them.
But they received for that at least a war.

Was a christian nation never taken formerly
{ *Or, not more than any other* },
But was fought for, died for by its people.
Were most wars waged for less.

When quickly overpowered, Kuwait,
As quickly was championed by fraternal states united...
Assistance speedily aiding the war. And more war.

How strange it is to see the warlike nation neatly overrun...
Hung petard the passive canard termed piety.

Is **needed** *land! for those with none!*
Is always need of place...
Yet shall never warfare solve the land-use question put to Arthur...
Charge confronting from antiquity, the coronated line of kings.

{ ***Gone ignored, the fundamental premise....***
Find it addressed at the end of these essays! }

To die no better death than meted any tanus proving treacherous,
Pendragon lived Artanus.

Nor by any hand served mind-detached, that felled him...
The hand belonged to Mordred, murderer was his son.)

(Tanus anagramts to Satan.
Should who else create one ?)

BOOK TWENTY-TWO

WARS EVEN UNTO THE CRUSADES

The Legend of The Holy Grail,

Tale was rightly mine, adopted line and chapter.
Vestigial prop and popelarized:
Buttress relegated Roman doctrine:
Absorbed Mere afterthought Maide Maudlin
A trophy anecdotal hanging Glastonwydyn, an anemic acquisition:
Appurtenance procrustean trimmed Diminut-Io! Abbassare.

The centuries elapsing,
Ubiquitous and effulgent loomed demon relic the Baphomet
Ensconced The Word breathed encephalophonic inside its militent war head,
Proposing Crus-de-Sades far-flung, Grand-Master-Mind maneuvered
Easily triumphant his red-cross blooded papal banners...
Inspired the Inquisition, spent zealot passion for the cross...
Charged and found them paganscum the heathenscum heredics...
Auto-da-fé'd... Blessé'd...
And hotly burned them.

Policed the world. Beknights indeed! bent fealty such masters....
Known them by the guled and blooded crosses mantled on white field
Proclaimed of chastity and poverty...

Engaging in the ritual was occult and secret,
Were introduced monk-warriors, to consecrated helms their orders,
Revering them oracular,
Knights Templars once of High Degree Hierarchic;

Tradition ancient in its substitution of adored most Holy Relic,
Prize the very highest... temple was the former head
Of prophet died beheaded, the baptist was St. John.

(*Bequeathed on whom that terrebilis now? Serves it where?*)

The Knights Of Templared Head,
Initiated ass decaying plated D'aurum,
Niched as deity and templed...
Embraced and kissed third testa caput-menta,

Were tumbled! golden temples in the lock in keiss:
Tumblers sworn the baissé bouse! the Templars!
Loch and tumblars testis... tested tittilare osculum,
Opened access sacret crypts were men once like themselves,
Heirs-companionate new-alive partook of euxhristic f'ormulæ
Believed bestowed æturnal life,

Engendered wealth le fin de mortal fear...
Created Bourse, baise currency exchange: the kiss.
With time enough, provisioned the guerdon kund-aligning power....

Garnered D'Orme The Oroboursely!
Possessed of wealth enormous!
Knights of The Head were Templars.

Monks sullam ' What ails thee uncle? ' Mongralloy?

Hu-Mana-Tie betrayed (took but single instance),
Become no more than tale of pin the donkey on the tailings.
(Hu, the Dove, and Tiy, other goddess name for Life and Io Manna-
Calfed Her Isle of Mana, Dove and Coowed amuck across Bosphorous!)

Might even gold be found in bodies human She has Maide...
A vining similar to snaking och-ores veined Her Urth.
Well. Gold.... You do not find it easily of yourself.
(So how do onagers worshipping gold proceed,
Create and harvest their plantations...
When tide their civilization betrays and beggars them?)

Bullion masters, but coming all to grief Molay, Flamel et compagnie,
Finding too Inquisortive! Old Testesmentrix!
Latter-day we see survival and success now proceeding hand in hand:

Children House of Wroth have done it;
Descendant Frank won field proved worth its laine,
And Celtic Llew Law Hu-an, proved prototype of Frank en-tre-pan-neur
(French Lyon and Leydon, Caer Lisle township, his namesakes all).
Did fathom each of these, uncharted wisdoms of the brain.

Was Henry inventor young hotspur, first forded on wheels firing four,
Carted new buggy, a superior sort of mechanical horse,
And faster by far than the cow.
(Nor demanding asset aurum gold be rendered liquid fuel:
Unlimited oil, cheap crude, would do.)
Transpired that Seven Sisters Oil Cartel was to underwrite the evolution,
Build interhighway super boon - and abetted prime-time picto-raptor,
Mass Medea Mad Pan Optim, would oil sales net new garner further:
Glut spewing near-immortal Her Forms Immortal, Astarti!
Endless captured and coerced the lock of twisted starlight,
Is flow of oil Urth's blood, pulse its beat organic Grave-Ur Life,
Degraded nigh-forever by alchemick trick molds solids new A-poly-plast!

Easy the grant of plastic franchise guarantees an override bananza
To played out private province, republic is oppressed and over-regulate:
Oh! Soon be coffered gold again!

(First Maide Our Lady, Three-Eyed Io,
The world's Tres Yeuse rejoicing { their fate to bleed } ...
The dawn Dia.n.ai Luciferous announced her morning...
Bright Venus, rising Goddess of the night.)

Wink eyes publiminal Tela Vise Pan Opteyes,
Malagrandize net-worked link-up
Metamorpheuseyed the new Medea;
Who wins at last, by channeled flicker aegis,
The wars ubiquitous populust fanned whomo-sex and violtense
By bi-panderous vassals assophomoric... plus spy remained as ever,
Argus, surveillant sweeps unsleeping his cyclop lens electron,
Creating semblance like to ancient water spring, pulsing, bubbling
Glassy focus of the papule poisoned at the source its networked river.
Belching. Rheuming. Eructing phosphorescent bilge induced stagnation
In the common mind browsed pacified on swill sluiced dreary underground.

(Mongering warred before, Irackurr middle world was ancient Medes...)

Yet Medeam encephalic gone one better:
Captive tied and seated willing - gluts each man before her -
Drinking of æffluvia flooding forth his dwelling.
Resembles most, old formula exorcistic, the howl of scream and wailing.
So fisticate! preys the image
Plys its trade unmerciful
Bathos would press the world its service,
Bully by threat is scarce contained in legal jargon. Nota Bene!

Updated gadget, wired electron,
No less than Talking-Head Interrus,
Harangue and rhetorick its Net Wirld Highway.

Would seem proffered in-terr-tanus,
Mal-panoprop and propaggrandis
Persuasion more than equal to the goose!
(*The one which* **lays!** *the golden eggs.*)

Moongilt gilded,
No pretense the goddess served is other than herself...
Subsumed so easily Medea, by apollunic forces:
Subservient his will.... The Set, A Dora.

See how surely all are drawn the rim of vortex.....
Clutched you once... would never let you go.

For you I seek safe overlook
From seethe and boil of cauldron's bore,
But protection overcome and unsuccessful,
Begets adversity penaltimate.

BOOK TWENTY-THREE

MARY THE STUART, ELIZABETH TUDOR

Last time, stood fair the wind from France
For Mary, Queen of Scots,
And their iron grasp blown with it,
Her family was De Guise:
Defenders anyone should dazzle;
Leaders of the armies of the former king
And appointments stellar within the catholic church
Were ranking princes still.
Despite was lessened their pernicious influence,
No nearer its attainment that simplicity was agrarian peace
Offered first such gentle promise, came legacy the ancient goddess line.

Once had seemed was nearly so....
Little Marie, as all who knew her called her then,
Endeared herself to most of those existing powerful at court,
Maide plain to all she was sans doute beloved by Francois,
Dauphin, eldest son of Henry II King of France,
And ' Italian Woman ' Catherine was his Queen (scion of House Medici).
Fanned lively flame her merry humor, restored was gloomy royal house,
Revivified by gaiety played so youthful, yet ever decorous its grace...
By idylls sprung the sweet Arcadian
Bloomed pastoral breath anew.

Then circumstanced upon the death of Henry, King of France,
Life bestowed indulgence further, on new young king was Francois II
And his winsome wife of sixteen summers:
Profusely showered by rich adornment,
These royal heirs who wielded rule its full possession,
Bright lustre gleamed vermeil did represent The Valois Throne of France.
Howsobeit, dreaming in enjoyment of so heavenly, their eden;
They would abide but fleeting season, that singular, glorious year.

Never lay so close before, proximity to Paradise,
Nor seen before that lambent joy played lucent over innocence...
Reigning careless ease on peoples' pleasure,
Loved them and delighted in them.
Did indulge her fondest fancy - young Marie;
Granting freedom in their hearts and minds to all,
Inventing disports pastoral for their bodies.

(*Not truly a Society The Feminine, all life known cherishing equal,*
Maide access easy to abundance of the fruitful earth.
But all the same, did spirit rule was generous,
Howsoever was confined by economy squeezed oppressive,
Underwrote expenditures of the militant-political,

Was bound by dominance and canon, infallible religion;
Essentially those restrictions established and enforced,
Upheld supremacy presumed the masculine.)

But a year, in short, for both of them,
Meant Paradise.

Would end.

Never stout, his health to fail.
And not to live beyond the year, her dearest friend,
Young Francis.

Ruthless cast aside. Shunted off to Scotland, Mary;
Deported back again to bleakness never hitherto conceived.

Queenship once ruled Paradise
Must now address new school of John, Hard Knox.
Gotterdammerung the mission; his delight, to chivy and harass her,
Bludgeon merciless quotation delivered hugely slanted
By-gotry in service of phan-testes waxing evermore selective,
Purported issued doctrine true Bi-Gott! supported by biblical text!

Meanwhile descended Rule Disorder further, over continent was Europe.
Although would forge her islands, England, unite them as one kingdom,
An oppressive yoke of hegemony long enjoined by The Roman Catholic Church
And dominant the centuries was in the end abolished.

And religion flourished next that country, High-Anglican was protestant,
As Elizabeth Rex of England, sovereign queen and patron of the church,
Declared herself forever as its head.

As historically must Mary, Queen of Scotland (and its Steward),
Be forever defamed in the loss of hers.

By murder and by magic was eclipsed the looped alliance,
Genetic cables linking Houses Sewert and Lawre-Reine....
Strands Merovin La Grande Femille, defused and feckless in fret again,
A significance shrunk mundane.
Sunk to petty plot abysmal. Wastrels adrift on the waters occult.
To live suppressed or gone to ground the true and Holy Family,
Root and and Branch of Goddess line.

Always would the four inveigle,
Not simply two contending parties for control of Western Worlds...

First: The Catholic Pope of Rome, ikon infallible headed his Church,
Whose military arm effected full delivery of the potent message:
Retainment and exercise perforce of temporal and eternal power
Fast secured by the militent mandate pronounced as Christ's.

Then secondly, those apostates and renegades,
Themselves collateral branchings
Of the mighty tree of DNA was Maide Diana.

Had these installed themselves like eggs deceiving,
Came unwelcome cuckoo bird,
Then cradled and protected by the arms not quite androgynous
Of Mother was all-powerful was their Mother Church:
Would plot and burrow her demise,
Destroy from within as first taught them the termite.

Concurrent these The Hidden Third: safe foot astraddle in both camps,
Sustained by belief unshakeable that the best must always win -
It did but serve with equal canny - earthly god Mammon and God Jehovah.

How many centuries been expended before succeeded that accomplishment?
Well. Protocols essayed such dreams as these sought capture of eternity.

Seeming always had existed expansive sweep of Holy Empire,
Its overseer the Catholic Rome.
Now encountered protestant incursion and rising of hostilities,
Was forced its shedding piece by piece, concession dismantled unwilling,
That seething fiefdom won so bloody, a mangled turf claimed holy ground.

But beyond and within those dual mainstreams of belief,
There existed in a way, two popes: two vicars of religion:
One who wore Johannon's fishtail mitered hat,
Triple emblem pescatore of The Christ was Fisherman of Souls;

And dispensing influence esoteric the other,
His Order Fourth, the one most secret
Ensconced his lair and covert screen the mythical,
Safe dismissed to ' Realm of Fancy ',
That patriarch alleged afflicted:
The Maimed or Fisher King.

Famous his assertion was The Goddess his true mother.
Had appointed him D.n.asty Keeper of The Holy Grail.

Pah!

Remember the claim of one called Joseph... native to Arimathea,
Reported sat in elders' councils of Sanhedrin and was a wealthy man.
Also told was he apostasized - secret follower and disciple
Of the Nazarene was Jesus Christ,
That he would upon its crucifiction, take that body hence was so revered
And bury it in a private tomb lain within the garden was Gethsemane.

For his part in these affairs, it is told he was cast into jail,
And there appearing to him supernatural, the savior Jesus set him free;
Unlocked his prison cell - no need the key - did walk with him,
Conveyed to him Great Truth by whisper, secret word alone was Christ's.

Declaring inspiration thus, his charge,
He whisked them from the Hill Golgotha,
Provided escort for the family first meant Christendom:
Accompanied them the journey overseas to northern isles of Britain,
To be sequestered nearby Isle of Glass, outpost of monkish lay brothers,
Wherefore punitive concealed, would flourish no protection
Dispensed by human was so flawed was punished his moral defection.
Smote in the thigh, old libertine. A trait transmitted his line!
Yea! Even unto son (nephew some do say or was perhaps a grandson),
Was He-bron declared to be Bron.

Magdalen having embarked for France,
With children fathered by Je-Sus,
Identities all concealed, faced threat of persecution.
(Imperative the message of his death and resurrection
To substantiate the catholic cause...
But any further speculation on the family life of Christ
Was held calumny subverted catholic dogma pronounced and Maide anathema.)
Outlawed the children these! heretics charged with fraudulent existence.

While never much the mention of those were tunneled undetected,
Conspicuous posed as mighty pillars upheld its body, Holy Church,
Gone out murderous, mounted strike spilled blood of any were outside it.
The protestant summarily slaughtered and dispatched the harmless jew
By warrant sworn the perfidious lie, deposed conspiracy of displacement,
Be it by the hand of agent, or any other so misguided
As to swear its fealty to family bore The Holy Blood.

(Flying once, inside a dream of time I sent,
You reached your destination lay eastward on the eastern hills,
A shephard's hut that housed Wise Ancient,
Keeper of the Archives termed Akashic.

He it was to sound the warning, " Do not let them see you fly!
Else they will shoot you down and ground you. "

Somewhere on Caunce, the street meant paveéd,
Winging strong between Elizabeth and Bu-Chanon,
You were seen by others: forced down pilots **had no eyes!**
Who with only empty gaze to guide them were proceeded on sad foot,
Backs set against the east, blind stumblers struggled indifferent tides.
Yourself inexplicably and suddenly pedestrian,

Wrestled upstream like some spawning salmon
Against discarded militant and sightless dregs, humanity;
Sentenced yourself immutable labor, earth bound just as they.
Oxlike toiled so long in that condition it might have been forever!

You thought at first their sightless sockets
Meant they had ' cried their eyes out '.
But dreams you must remember, serve the function of projection:

Incarnate lifetimes served before you knew whose eyes!
They could have been no other's than the ones had been your own!
Ultimately rebound upon you, beat you, pavé you down!)

He it was, Buchanan,
Who first was champion and protagonist of Mary Stuart.
Become convinced of her consent to bloody murder of her husband,
Co-regent, the former Henry Stuart (another born of Tudor clan,
Who was the Earl of Darnley, son of Matthew Stuart, Earl of Lennox);
Contrived those plots paved way for Elizabeth the Tudor,
Remove from Grace and bring poor Mary Stuart down.
Between them grounded! Landed head the block between them!
Their tender ministrations!

Had all England clamored for that Scottish Mary's royal head:

What likelihood retain it,
Possessed so uneasy her anglican throne,
Beleaguered Queen and Helmsman, Elizabeth who was England?
Risen most of catholic Europe, the revolt against the protestant,
And rival Mary Stuart's family, the hated catholic De Guise
Would scourge and massacre triumphant,
Both Huguenots and heretic, and any professing to protestant.
Was even Gloriana in receipt of papal bull anathema;
A discretion seemed at most but sanction for her murder.

Alone to be sustained was sovereign island realm was Albion,
Protestant quarry evaded capture, foxing its predator, papist Rome.

Yet no royal author penned it,
The formal mandate ordering Mary Stuart's execution.
The claim is made that such decree did override the wish of Majesty,
Elizabeth fell to swooning horror at grievous news received
Of death of Sister-Queen and royal cousin.

Beheld that pitiful relic, head was Mary's!
Horror indeed! ' Cried its eyes out. '

Fruit of Grape and Vine descending,
Bore the wine, great blood...
Pawn tendered forfeit the blood-money savage!
For infamous thrones!

BOOK TWENTY-FOUR

FLED OLD WORLD FOR NEW AMERICA

Unfurls within the memory synchronistic that is mine,
That field chronistic is the narrow stage of human story -
Overview of all and everything gone dignified as ' history '.

Yet no chronology this, concordance confirming the world's!
No. Related are Merely peregrinations, Maide the Grail's travail,
While is nowhere included the traverse to come.

When split The Royal Vine of France,
Sought collateral stems effete and weakened
The creation of New Fronde.
Powerful still at court,
Advised by frère ecclesiastic politically mute,
Third generation oenclés fomented civil chaos,
Then abetted further by offshoots were the dukes Lorraine.
Cousins cadet to the Guise.

(*Viticult abused by graft too often, strung mutant fret and stop -*
Root and grapple wilted vitiate, sapped impotence inoperable.)

But throughout the century was fifteenth, contenders struggling all,
As sought control of House Valois, the possession, its royal seat.

But twenty years would see it slip their grasp
As princely heir is born to Louis, Thirteenth King of France.
What matter then that younger brother, D'Orleans,
Was wed Joyeuse de Couiza?
Flowed Parisian streets already,
Blood royal running factioned veines of holy blooded families
Sang ancient claims of Sangre Divine that coursed the life first mine.

Nightwalkers now must flee headquarters of their secret underground,
War theater long abandoned, bivouac foreseen Fraternity so ardennet,
First inspiring foray carried populist...
New-age birth emergence from dense forest cradle was Stenay....
Yet treads again its center-stage! some thread of fronded bloodline,
Settling province known Arcadia in continent new world was Canada.
(*Resurrected relegated ' Cajun ' as Arcadia turned into ' Arkadi '.)*

Among the leaders, new arrivals, hied one was best of Norman stock...
(*Singular pride of innkeep wealthy, Pierre LeMoyne was his sire -*
Plied wealthy trade the bourgeoisie in northern port of French Dieppe.)
Found himself embarassed by political and civil press,
Had fled perforce in darkness, bid adieu bienville, good hometown,
To disembark first outpost, safe haven the new Americas.

Was earliest among them, that suave Fraternité des Gentilhommes,
And known soon to Canada, Charles LeMoyne, as l'homme plus formidable!
Politico shrewd and adept... most personable of traders...
Interpreter fluent the Indian tongues... Le Grand Msr. Le Moyonner.

Entrepeneur notwithstanding, truth was: the loyalist still,
Devoted to those authors of the phase came next the Fronde,
And confidante of His Grace, Le Duc de Longueville of northern France
(Grandchild of Louis de Gonzaga, the Italian Duke de Nevers,
Befriended alchemist and esoterica. Claimant of The Blood).

In times of peace
(Term signified no more than lack of formal war declared),
The early turbulence of settlement amongst those dismissed as savage,
Meant strange and dismal study of attrition in the wilds.
Gentlemen tyros failing all, at first...
Bushrangers, then attaining chieftainships of lawless, roving gangs:
Proscribed at times by government, at times conspiring with it,
Desperadoes leagued together in traffic of the dubious, the contraband.

Slowly to rise the lowliest ranks of those who mastered the fur trade,
Craft requiring divers skills and one to prove most lucrative.

Yet paramount... were Gentlemen all,
And reduced to meanest circumstance, their lives....
Possessing no position real or formal, nor certainty of upkeep,
They enjoyed no more preferment than did any other social cipher.

Though personage different, was this one:
Attaining eminence in New Canada,
Founding father of the family which produced a mighty line;
First Governors of Canada and other sundry province,
Discoverers and explorers of its waterways the awesome Mississippi
Sailed them down and bore them south
To territories were tropical and vast,
Where young ensign named them Louisiana, after Louis, King of France;
Creating next that city honoring royal brother, the Monsieur D'Orleans.

Great host of statesmen-traders supporters public of the king and pope,
Reasonable was their expectation to share rewards of French expansion,
Laboring howsoever unbeknownst the pursuits of their own interests,
Those persons cultivated God Jehovah as much as Earthly Mammon,
Laid down seeds of insurrection would undermine both Church and Goddess;
Implanted revolutionary stance conspired replace or overthrow the old.
(Family. Bloodline Holy. And any other claimant reckoned potent.)

And should be thought that first Arcadia to have revived,
There would not again be introduced a cult of Womens' Goddess!
And could in no religious mission therefore prosper, Brothers Marist.
Compromised is Virgin Merey. Her name is rallied uneasy.
And howsoever worshipped by the populous as tenet of Catholic creed,
The benevolence of their goddess was soon de-emphasized!
No country this, so vastly wild and rugged
To be settled by worshipful milksops!
No. Required were rugged men to match!

Redolent of the foreign... soldier retained his air exotic,
Phenomenal his ascent, the Charles LeMoyne,
Jesuit now turned trader.
Expanding steady acquisition, tracts of land provided fief and dower,
Secured them noble futures as multiplied his princely brood...
Granted him were letters of nobility: Charles, Le Sieur de Longueuil:
Titled in perpetuity, all his house.

And thoughtful ever of their interests in the dialects were their own,
He was to browbeat natives unexposed and ignorant -
Roamers feckless, mostly nomad, led by greed for gain of bauble,
Or pricked caprice of curiosity, however mild its form -

To embrace of new and barbaristic creed
Pledged same salvation as accorded mystic resurrection
Of the paleface sky-god Jesus.
Hung his cross and crucified the Savior.

Établissement de la Foi:
Extravagantly esteemed were conversions of the heathen....
Credit all redounding to that sophisticated glory,
The white man's Mother Church.

(*Remained a factor of significance not heretofore revealed:*
Were bred in the bone and determinate in the genes,
Significs spelled the name LeMoyne...
French meanings indicated equal;
Moi, Moyen, Moine and Moin:
First fashioned I, the ego,
Then manager and provider
Follows after lay-monk, a verb unlikely, to lack.
Explains preamble this,
Its spiral ascent the alpha beta dendron tree,
Columnar coded mysterious script,
Devised and Maide as The Grail:

Grafted that same line and flourished,
Again descends the ladder bears him reincarnate,
First man alive was Ladan.
And in these the so-called latter days,
He will call her spirit to himself,
Messenger ancient, newly risen,
Newly spelled her latest version,
The Lady D.N.A.)

Proud flew the English flag on Canada.

Indian League and tribes of aborigine played off against each other,
Winning bloody victories in the wars against themselves,
Nought else served but division of alliance with the French.

History this:
Caused citizen of French Canada
To anglicize his name perforce as English subject...
Adopt the Britons' speech,
To accept excessive war taxation...
Be massacred.... Or get out.

Nostalgia rising from these times
The songs and legends Cajun...
Staggering exodus long after,
Last reach Louisianan shores....
Longfellow (Longeueil is anglicized),
His sad journal penned immortal
Those migrations fruitless were Evangeline's,
Heart star-crossed and faithful,
Tracked pursuit a lifetime,
Seeking her childhood Arcadian lover.

Now divested of their lands,
The erstwhile arms of throne was France -
Raised to zenith,
Fallen nadir, the issue of Longeueil.
Governors and sons, the Sieurs D'Iberville,
Le Moyne and De Bienville,
By their king so treacherous... impeached,
Then indifferent: shot for treason!
While years must languish some, awaiting death in jail.

After but one century and a second quarter mark,

Cast aside and ruined ignominious, Les Sieurs de Bienville.
Near extinct that family of settlers,
Were first Governors of Canada!

As would royal, but unseemly relish,
Disenfranchise them altogether -
Send them down the River Mississippi
Trading Indians -
No more possessed than these of education,
With even smaller comprehension!

All that Mississippi delta,
Colonies so undervalued, territory so fertile,
Then exchanged by Charles the Third,
In trade accomplished sleight of hand.
The deeds transferred, from France to Spain...
Wiped them clean, the spendthrift's kingly debts at home.

Such recognitions further fed that bonfire was The Fronde,
Sparked France again that century...
And within the hundred years lay hence (commencing 1789)
To be ignited bloody Revolution.

Remember how was told you fronded factions
Contended with the Holy Family?
To act in fact same case with everyone?
Here we have example of the French and royal line
(Whose boast was sacred blood-tree),
Stamping out and bleeding out
(In Holy Family Name),
All those jealous of the right to Holy Rule
Had descended from The Goddess... She who was The Mother.

Be he Catholic or protestant,
Fisherman Pope, or fissure man but maimed -
Not one amongst them strove restore the Mother's rule.
Indeed. Reviled it and defied it.

Doctors brilliant, of the Church
(Take their name hirudo from the leech),
From templar knights sworn poverty,
To nun was meek and humble,
Served crumbled pillars one and all
Apollo, Prince of Earth:
Children leached again hirudo.

BOOK TWENTY-FIVE

RUSSIAN SAXE-COBURG - (*GOL*) - GOTHA

Then a century more were come again,
Those descendants mine and Ladan's.

(*Is told of them before*
As hailing French community
The good-town, Bienville.
Conveyed The Bien né that these were keyed wellborn.

{ *While translates the word for ' hail '*
As ***grêle*** *in French,*
And does line of Grail derive from same sound Holy.
Then sings the sangre sacred further,
German word is ***Heilig.*** *})*

Victorious was the work.
Maide L' Oeuvre very first,
Those cradled eggs,
Time-cycles lain their Mothering Church,
The boned and pelvic girdle
Created venus shell and blessed chalice.

Mine the task of fashioning gamete shelter,

Form used and structured the **Dome Egg-Lys***,*
Curve revering of that womb did gracious serve as living Church,
Bore lily shaped her Grand Graal and bassin...
Maide of herself the human DNA;
Built and carried calc and skele,
Scaffold very prototype and replicate Our Image.

Utters high, new mode the living word,
Translates virgin sound to substance
Delivering from her virgin womb the loving Merey,
New vowels Maide enunciate, sound descending spiralled
To enter worlds become the flesh;
Muttherings softly circled resonate,
Maide you New Harmonic, Chaliced Grail,
Potter formed you all.

Yet pitted and eroded as by devils in a sandstorm
Lay every marbled softness that streaked its human clay;
Vital flesh and plotted over aeons was further blurred the melting pot
To fuse the lines crossbred -
Producing progeny grown coarsened,
Obscure its source and definition.

Degraded over centuries,
Those first familial skeins Maide DNA.,
The threads engendering Nicholas Romanov,
Tzar Nicholas II of Russia,
And bred from same blood the German Alexandra,
Sad unfortunate who would become his wife.

(*One shared ancestry of Grail-blood with fated soul*
Was Mary Stuart, Queen of France and Queen of Scotland;
Grandchild most favored by Victoria,
Queen of England, Empress of The Commonwealth,
Who upon her darling's birth
Had dubbed her ' Sunny '.)

He who long ago was known as Ladan,
Again for deepest reasons of his soul,
Elected life incarnate.
(*Remember he was the template Maide original,*
Minne-human custom sized,
And proportioned for new earth-life Minni-planet.)

Assuming that imperial persona,

Nicholas, The Autocrat, Tzar of Russia,
He seemed unharried by same vexations
As were borne by Elizabeth Tudor,
England's Virgin Queen;
Who, compelled to engage in nonsensical cavil,
Refused any announcement of future succession,
Or make formal the naming, her designate heir.

To all appearance was Nicholas/Laden favored in domestic fortune;
More in question was his patriarchal role of Holy Father,
The servitor presumed of Russia's people,
The birthright holy revered....
He was instead enslaved by deference only supine:
Pivotal the adoration for whom he worshipped as his goddess,
Idolized and deified as if was Maide, Germanicus Grail...
Offshot sprung Holy the Vine's Sacred Blood.

(*Alas! No more to flicker, the inner goddess lambent.*
To the faith of Russian Orthodox converted,
Now is sacrosanct submerged...
Encompassed endless graft and intromission,
Do fundaments transmute to melancholic zeal perverted...

And metamorphize the morbid.
Progressive warp of monomania presumed itself infallible -
By orthodox and patriarchate church is unquestioned and upheld -
Assumes authority and privilege of Caesero-papist unaccountable:
Transforms itself to autocrat self-deified.
The God sent.

{ *No longer ceded to the romish popes is the fealty of empire.* } *)*

Disavowed - or possibly misprized
The primal clamor of his soul,
And hallowed genes in his case were overruled:
For was deity alone, his Sunny,
To engage his heart, his head.

Nicholas/Ladan's former oath declaring dedication to Diana,
Was worth proved little more than imitative epigonic...
Reduced to but the temporal,
Dimensions of his earth perceived...
A focus wholly comprised of the kingdom of men.

This was the time that salic law prevailed in Russia....

And for lack of son and heir tsarevitch
(None but daughters followed after),

Or any other Romanov was appropriate, not deceased,
Then scrutinized the multitudes' focus,
Affixed in public and pitiless glare,
Must Nicholas contemplate himself perforce,
As emperor coming last his line of Romanov;
Span of dynastic rule enduring three hundred Russian years.

Last of the breed was certain...
Sovereign exalted the absolute monarch.
And condition lay undreamed the constraint of formal constitution.

Had confronted no serious challenge heretofore
The royal fortune so prodigious;
And known no want or lack of any sort,
Russia's throne supreme.
Yet a heritage unsecured by masculine heir of his natural body,
Rendered them unstable, the prospects of his sovereign portion,
Effecting their despair, his royal wife and children,
That their long familiar and imperial mode,

Might not indefinite continue.
So finite in scope their foreseeable future:
The vista appalled them.

Five times would Alexandra labor,
Serve hence the cause of heritage:
To bear, hard case, her guarantee at last,
The son was braw and bonny,
Welcome heir the royal Russian male child,
Great-grandchild to the British Queen, Victoria.

(Gift gone ignored, or overlooked,
The hemophiliac blood that gouting savage,
Did not clot, invaded tissue unimpeded,
Pooled cavity and artery which veined the tender flesh?)

Six weeks she lived for joy,
New mother pampered her man-child;
Task paramount accomplished, her term to bask as wife approved.

Awful receiving the warning:
That simplest of bruises might kill him.

(The leys disrupted....
Destabilized the overlays that networked human flesh.
Vine of ancient blood so holy,
First Blood the Maiden Grail,
Spews malediction bacteritic now,
A rampage-fate leads mortal...
Blood unstaunched that weeps accursed in goutings vile.
Visitant is invisible that wields its strike on boy-child...
Genetic gift descending tragic from the female is his mother.

{ Should wish create The Line of Maide anew, unblemished...
Needed mastery indeed such alchemy, to fuse afresh its crucible. })

For the newborn's hemophilia, came no prognosis providing of hope.
Scarce sufficient was knowledge to manage.
And no more than empty exercise, the discussion any cure.

Condemned this hapless royal kin,
To undergo his fateful suffering with him,
Perchance endure its lifetime.
While he in turn despising them, learns the cherishing of hate.
What to do?

The disposition of that question,
Has changed the world and history....

Disease which lurked tzarevich's blood -
Upon its tragic advent was
Swift assigned the covert status of state secret.
And for disclosure any sort,
Needed those few sworn, were privy to it,
To contemplate the sentence for high treason.

Nicholas, as steersman at the helm of Russia,
Consistent with expedience
Employed the use of daily cover-up,
Attempted navigate his craft of state
Across morass of propaganda...
Misprision compounding further,
Arisen omission of truth.

Yet blessed by sometime grace,
Before must fray those seams of trust
Sustained the Royal Circles... supported them...
Maintained them icon in the hearts of Russian peoples.

Erratic the heartbeat determined the empire;
Pulsation lacked foresight its fate.
Unstable the heart so constant confronted,
The prince-child fought foe was his death.

And all must endure the ravage his anguish;
Permitted no surcease, those near him,
Sharing the life of the suffering boy.
His days and his nights shriekings strident,
The fever-wild prayers groaned aloud...
Prayers beseeched but of death.

Life for the nurse his imperial mother,
Scrolled nightmare its horror unending.
Came never physician relieving...
One to realize full scope of horror.
Might any time of day or night befall its impact,
Occur the accident so innocent for all others,
Yet circumstance to him meant ecstasy of tortured tissue
Bloody burst the veins, then vied for place with bone.
She, who helpless clasped his hand and wiped the pallid brow,
Withstood each crisis stoic,

Would purchase oh so slowly, fleet stay of armistice too brief
Marked tortured truce unknown its measure, defined hiatus only.

(*Concerning the matter and status of heir,*
They lived as bunkered soldiers lived:
Tended their wounds... awaited new missile....

The difference was, a war conducted clandestine...
So dire concealed and ill-advised.

Such was the household and flagship the realm.

A breach of truth set ultimate seal to Russia's fate....
Indeed, was toppled western Europe.
Changed course all rule the familiar world. Forever.)

It happened there appeared at court a Russian holy man;
Those there were would recognize, salute him as the Staret.
But only the roustabout infamous crude...
Peasant was low and was cunning...
Bad monk the preachings Priapus,
Mad braggart Gregori Rasputin.

No right sound was made,
Yet obtained was the Empress' ear.

Prostrate lain so often, set isolate in pain,
Came opportune for young tsarevich,
That mystic gift of healing
Reached out to hand and cradle rocked the throne!

Perhaps he was adept hypnosis, the monk Grigori;
He was assuredly magnetic.
And irrefutable the bounty of his power
Sprung animal vitality and boundless constitution....

Those to meet him from the very first
Confirmed the gaze so deep had mesmerized....

(Excused it thus their embarkation
Shared bizarre, erotic course?)

Swept in spate the eminent healers
Through the corridors of the palace,
And even so was every other avenue explored.

Yet alone might Rasputin pacify,
Quell wrack of princeling's pain...
And salience of this mercy constant every crisis
Engendered royal gratitude within her frenzied breast
The Empress Mother hitherto distraught.

She esteemed him God's anointed...
Angelic divine destined save them...
Sentiments howsoever were exalted would override all others.

To pronounce him openly to empire, ' Our Friend ', the royal couple.
Irrevocably aligned with rank familiar grown too close.
Would not be long before was felt and heard the spider spit!

Yet proportionate to this, smoldered ripping discords of disquiet:
A populace incensed its every order
By this notorious and unholy ' Father '...
By the infamous iniquity initiated sexual congress,
With himself to play their mentor, self-styled holy priest -
While purported fornication such
To offer them redemption in the sight of God:
Fiend had rampaged conquest without limit!

Was society of all degree embroiled in common,
Had so great a part of it too wildly flouted ancient decency.
Appearing once again high-minded, howsoever smothered unrepented,
Panted hot the awful guilts suppressed,
As were at last unloosed those masked and feral angers,
Maide charge... howled wolf...
' Complicity at court '...

Which, providing growing revelation of further truths withheld
From those with civic right to know...
Dreamed unaware and ignorant of the gathering alienation...
Spun compromised and rudderless drawn down in yawning vortex.

(Lie here the seeds of Russia's dissolution.
Germination inexorable gone unrecognized...
Toxic blossoms thriving fractal, rising rooted darkness....)

Though always he might soothe, Rasputin could not cure
The chronic nature of disease laid waste the royal blood
Ran fatal race against longevity:
Indeed effected penultimate threat to Russia:
Destabilized its throne.

Insistent on the protocols of secrecy,
Intelligence within the household
Was not to offer explanation as regarded mystic status
Of its increasingly secular monk -
Neither as to role of comforter who eased the young tzarevich,
Nor that indulgence issued royal enclave...
Manifest how ill-conceived!
A situation insupportable... and yet... and yet...
It must be borne.

How ensure succession else for child lacked health to rule,
Enduring life so frail and indeterminate of tenure?

Far worse. Was ever the tsarevich properly assayed,
And a candidate favored more robust,
Alexei would likely be put aside...
The imperial futures with him.
What then? Oh what then?

As single shield between them and conceivable exilement,
Stood yet staunch that gentleman...
Beleaguered emperor of a nation was entered even then in war.

Not that it posed the personal threat.
Not likely it would kill him...
And yet... and yet... he was their sole insurance.
Not even Friend Gregorovich could stay the mortal tides.
Caller of the storm winds, he was instrument to further them.

Base scandal would finger the very throne of Empire;
Vilified was sad Czarina as ' The German Woman '.
A populace translating thus her German birth
Pronounced her foreign spy who harbored alien sympathy.

For this was how was read, ' the aloofness of her heart '
That hid from them the core of her existence:
Considered everywhere as cold disdain
The preemption of concern for all that lay beyond the famous boudoir
(Swathed the favorite mauve
Denoted second year of mourning to the English),
Accommodated mercifully private,
The recurrence her Golgotha...

For Alexei embodied calvarian cross to her,
The cross whereon she hung with him,

Child who suffered, lived tortured.

Become so fearfully unpredictable,
And impotent just as much
The youngster's hands wherein reposed
The weakened threads of empire.

Bound such conditions of conspiracy and morbidity so covert;
Parameters shifted constant flux that held the royal secret,
A greater threat to her than posed from any rank outsider.
Let them murmur treason! Was she not in fact
The Empress of The Russias? Highest of the church?

And yet... and yet...
There lay the shadow.
Accused, might not defend herself:
Meant silence to her, their common survival.

So multilayered its depths, was concealment worse by far
Than any possible surmise of nation kept unwitting.
Seemed no far step to couple her name (and person)
With scoundrel... was louche Rasputin.

And of aspersion such as that, what might she say?
Her lover? Too ridiculous!
And how condone corruption in which she would never believe?

But crying shame!
The people's indignation hungered for its quarry
Who delivered them his practice,
Did fornicate so heinous with his advocate, The Devil.

Did she so, or did she no...
Increasingly seen his dependent,
Constant raven preened her presence.

And if not sufficient, that,
Was disapproved his loose carousal in the taverns,
Where vainglorious of his power within the Russias' court,
Spat innuendo spewing lewdness passed beyond the treasonous.

We know of her dependency.
However should be other than was viewed
There did exist most truly,
The form of blackmail impressed her into service,

Flat requisite so stark,
Perforce must rely on staret's constant intervention...
Continue foster the illusion that Alexei Nicholaievich,
Future heir of Russia, was possessed of normal health.
Failing this. Where were they?

The wars they had engaged in... not to prosper.
Excess only wanton that underwrote the armies:
Squandered men and money. Two more bloody years.
Oh... were rumblings loud the corridors.

Not quite to send him mad, scenes Byzantine his court,
Yet no longer could he countenance, this Czar,
The practice of deceit had plunged him to perdition,
Had sunk him whorl of vortex ever deeper,
Degraded his wife as ' The German Whore '.

Despite the protests of his several ministers,
Did Nicholas then decide to spend his time away,
Assume the leadership his armies
And take the ten year old and heir apparent,
Their son Alexei with him.

An event to prove disaster!
It seemed but minor head cold caused him violent to sneeze:
Yet his blood did brightly flow unchecked,
His temperature begin its steamy rise.
Obvious was no other course -
But return Alexei to his home,
Provide him proper nursing....

Arriving weak and failing,
Wrappings bloodied endless changed as fresh bled each removal:
Could scarce imagine, anyone,
An end to prove so near...
But his strengths declined progressive,
Warning any moment he could die.

In the end despairing,
Defiant of her husband's known displeasure
Regarding all related to unholy priest:
' *For Baby's sake ' she humbly sent for him,*
Man so many ways had shamed her,
Yet whose presence granted benediction, surcease;
Upon her soul bestowed relief.

Nicholas retreated to his legions:
Persisting inaccessible within the barracks.

Then! How quick to make it clear!
She it was, would govern!

Does after this, Ratsputin,
Attain to fullest political strength:

Advisor-Leech, parasite the leach field
(*Clings to Russia's Little Mother,*
A character reminiscent, revenant perhaps was Cling-sore)...
Corruption burrowed body politic even deeper than before.
Stage set the advent of hell.

Offenses were too long, too many
To pacify his subjects' hearts that harbored only vengeance:
For perdurance of negligence and bloodbath,
For flouted trust and expectation,
For indifference shown apparent
As was always placed before them
The welfare of his family.

(Were not ***all****, his Russian children ?)*

For the influence unsuitable
Was wielded by The German Whore, his wife,
Which she then extended to her paramour.
Why! Even denied them was sight and presence
Of the bonny princeling they worshipped as their own!

But case by itself. Calamitous...
Was the contempt revealed by royalty
Demonstrated martial power so brutal,
It culminated in their massacre, one thousand Russian workers.
While received assault and injury some two thousand more.

Signal, that atrocity to ignite first rounds of revolution,
Sustain slow-fuse its ghastly prologue to that final coup de grâce.

Had whomsoever commanded military gunfire,
The army got its order, " Mow them down! "
The peasantry unarmed... milling... all unwitting.

Nicholas, in ignorance of coven and conspiracy

Meant covert mount of cannon fire on passive peasants
Peaceful gathered Palace Square...
Immediate was ensnared belief that he himself was target,
Intended victim of some anarchistic plot.
Taste not his first of violence proffered life and family,
But too intimate its breath, that spectre of assassination.

And a nation mourned their passing,
Would commemorate that day as Bloody Sunday.

Once their idolized Holy Father -
They baptized Nicholas henceforward, ' Nicholas the Bloody '.

Grim prophecy of the final days
Fomented revolution flared in 1917.

(Displayed by courtesy of an infiltrated Bureau of The Police,
Those bullet riddled portraits borne inscription unforgettable:

' The Tzar Cursed By The People '.)

* * *

This was where had led:
A nation splintered under revolutionists.
The reins of Autocrat so feebly relinquished,
Delivered the hands of interests disparate - pair was unfit, unworthy.
Mad for power the one,
Pathetic dupe the other.

Yet had neither one attained to zenith
Except for factor gone unreckoned,
The despotic child played puppeteer for whom they danced.

In face of mothering indulgence
A boy had learned the domination of his family:
Acumen ruthless, would master royal household,
Use against them fluctuation of disease,
Ensuing mood swing,
Bully cruel and calculate....

(*Long had Nicholas understood*
That Alexei ruled as tyrant in his home.
The misgivings felt toward the invalid his son
Amounted simply to dread.)

Woe to the nation!
Should occupy such, its throne!

But more than monk and more than mother,
The child did hunger after sovereignty:

Alexei it was to jerk their string,
Dream of coronation effected early rule.
And all being said - why wait?
Who knew how long might Nicholas Romanov retain his mandate?
Alexei could promise as their next true heir,
To be infinitely biddable - surpass the sire
Who proved himself so wayward in passivity,
Supine bowed before his wife.

Overwhelmed unconscionable,
Were the rulers of the country...
As sought autocracy in short,
One lacking dependable character.

Thought resulted from his illness, despotic disposition...
Veered rages alternated melancholia, thence subsided apathy?

Was innate the disposition and predictably unstable,
Disquieting to Nicholas, causing him profound unease...
Able less and less to exercise autonomy,
Receive cooperation from any one about him.
Lay animus undeniable between the son and father...
A great dislike between them.

* * *

Pressed rude from peasant families were fifteen million men!

Presenting human breast - too often, little more -
To artillery and aircraft deployed the German war machine.

Was spent and squandered the blood of nigh four million men!
For naught but lock of familial horns
Indulged by overlords the royal masters
Drifted bitterness of internecine strife.

Reckoning comes. Oh yes.
The time arrives to pay.
Unparalleled then such suffering!

(A century more of blood new-spilled
Will taint and stain them red,
Old steppes of endless Russia,
Territory accounted limitless,
Spanned East Europe reached to Asia.

And do augur Jewish Marx and Engels,
The fulfillment of those prophecies
Foretold so long ago at Patmos...

Storms and thunders Apollonian
That loom Apollocolypse unstoppable.
The millennium long awaited, its protocols were set.
And a world was Maide conscious of historical upheaval...

Disintegrating, Russia's Empire, all its satellites;
Appearing first the hungry Bolshevik and Communist,
Stalinist and Social Democratic Party.
Then arriviste came Hitler, also dreamed of Empire,
Blasted forth to bid his strike.
Conspirators next met Three Great Powers
Dividing and carving all Europe between them...

Ruin followed after Romanov.
Demoralized that nation must address itself as ' Comrade '.
And occurring yet in Germany the nightmare shame that will not go away.

For loss of established monarchy,
For religion summarily dismissed,
For loss of semblance any love of country,
Either government or tradition -
Was traded virtual comfort: the immutable atomic bomb.

Existences the monstrous...
Dictators were these masters...
We hardly need to name them
Those entered in the breach.
Nucleus hence destroyed: does balance collapse at the center,

Yet always are wound the dancing puppet threads
Jerked reflex of his hands unclean, their mentor.

Yes. Of course you know him, Lord of Darkness,
Engineered the fall of Russia.
Follows next: The World.)

Of Romanovs' passaging Dantean
Traversed reverse the earthly heaven
To reach their purgatorio -
Careening in down-spiralled circles
They convened at last the fateful cellar,
Chambered its gore, their ultimate hell.

Resolved was the matter of Russia by mayhem conclusive:

A common pit contained dismembered, the community their remains.
Or what must pass for them....
All on the Road to Four Brothers.

One station of the cross their way -
Frail hope implanted in their hearts -
Promised rescue, English Cousin Georgie (George was Rex the Fifth),
His country to provide them familial haven.

English Cousin indeed!
Advised by his Privy Council at their firm behest:
Rescind the offer! Shortest order!
British Monarch, Constitutional!

Scrutinized again, accursed strain Gol-Gotha:
A name should really represent the British!
So is named anew their compromised line:
Become The House of Windsor.

Stained by remnants of The Holy Blood windsorcerers' hands!

Descended this! Line stemmed Saxe-Coberg-Gotha!
(What Sexe Goathas around - comes around.)

Will come at last ill-fated roamers Romanov upon their own Gol-gotha -
And station last fulfilled:
Here they will be shot, stoved in their bloodied Russian heads -
Buried the hill new mecca reposing their Russian skulls.

Reached nearly to conclusion this very brief account
Details The Wanderings of The Grail.
Exists the chapter just one more,
Which soon shall be related.

We have learned how diffusion of The Sangre Real
Did undermine foundations of my world....

Shown here are those civilizations various
Were first infused The Blood:
Any one of them enhanced or sought its glory,

Attaining blossom greatest flower - so many.
Unfurlings sumptuous their brocade.
Brilliance so typical,
The Russian grandeur we have viewed:
Pinnacle of splendor, and zenith unsurpassed.

Yet so easy is deflected from crux and pivot of its axis,
Soul's consciousness abandoned, substituted secondary dream:

Of Judas Plots Compounded. Dispatches from Beyond. *

Beware the Tender Vine doth bear no grapes:
Foreshadows famine such as that,
The ending of your world....

Yea! All the little foxes.

* The Judas Compound, Joyce James.

BOOK TWENTY-SIX

CHILDREN DESCENDED OF TRISTRAM

(Do Talking heads lie next in store...
And comfort further,
A virtueless reality is virtual,
Oraclonig double-hits on internations' highway,
Led to latest virsion mediacrity,
The Holy Gold New Graal...
Craaled and sold as feed,
Products Maide humans' fiscal ranches...
Milked are kin as oxen, Io-Dummy milch-cows.)

Howsobeit, summoning heard, The Lily is born in western isles,
Creates herself on coiling sounds ascending The Dove-Line spiral.
To all of Hume it does concern: pray the messenger be heard!
A tale is so well written!

(Writers true breeds my dubble-lin stable,
Litterarts Incarnate Word...
And structure bears its traces still the dub-black gene pool
Descended Brittany blood came ancient family Dove-line,
Star-crossed Dub-line tree whence issued tragic Tristram.)

* * *

Born jambon cells the north bourne,
Borne my daughter to the north -
Bourne north by bus transported;
Legacy of jambe's long bonne near ruin,
Jammed and broken my little Marylebone -
Legacy of Jambes and black poulaye.

But arrived no nest the fledgling this -
Survival offered slight protection,
Against suffused esophagons that barely fended death.

I saw the child was mine lie weeping.
Smote my heart as heard her bloody whispered prayer
Rise the winds above the clouds.

* * *

Noter Damus:

Oh. Dear Love, Maman...
Life teaches much that overwhelms. Affords me fear....
Rises phantom shrouded filaments from grave of earth's sere fathom.

Despairing, wished their torment buried, stifled deepest,
Their single baleful sight denied.

Yet stele-fyled stocked a ladan cave the skull my own,
Burns salted cell the d'arque of head
Too thinly membraned over fontanel
Must burst torrential screaming through the terah -
Thin the veil in d'ark of night!
Repeating recollecting sanque'en songre of terrabyss:

A sister's limbs are torn asunder...
Grey, their pigmentation.
The child was drawn and quartered.
Eaten.

Arcane baal-full phagontized the flesh.
Borchury its kuntry. Rolling heads. The eyes....
I dream them so immediate,
Implacable dwellers hiding infant-mind:
Conceived them once a form of baby life unfinished,
Reproduced existence awaited body's further growth...
Thought of them as terorrbim detached their head.

It is not that I am repetitious...
There is impetuns perhaps,
Thinks not to show you all afrights...
But certain is there something central issued in the lilys fyeld....

D'arquening sky must ruminasce, deceipher secret of its bearth;
Tarry channeled sekuhlar adaft,
If it thought to study by tera-beam's Magicus Urn....

Yet perforce do I ask: Pro-vision: or Pro-Fission?
Dual come for-giving? Or dual come for-getting?

Child subjected sight of Terren-Sis,
Brutality untenable... wondrous not succumbed
Before the violence, convulsed its fright,
Small agoniste La Vie consorting with Victrix Death.

(Dove the Lily of The Isle first grew the iris lily tree...
Eye of the aisle led the blood-fed flowers...
Moon-guilt gilded, where seeing, was seen...
On very Eve humanity was Ma-mana damned!
Maide Eve-il! Mannawhyte A-dame de-manned.)

Impossible of description, how must live
Endured the thorn and threshing,
Abiding terromentum terafeme, tertian ailed and tarerpant...
Drooped abject before the roth of severed head Jontanas',
Baphomet planted bloody relic on its server:
Introduced as prototype decapitate,
As prophet witnessed scriedant spirit
Of the one beloved, he came before.

(Thought himself unfit to tie hus latchet!
Who cleansed and bathed him in the River Jordan.)

Crying still their wilderness,
Puissant heads de Capet-tête,
Rana-visaged terrus...
For wroth to come, the bloody raign of terror
Torn the branch and fronde en france... sown tares wild oat and Hote:

Shawn L'Haute and L'Eau alike, Lo! The Headeous Strength.
Food plattered patermost for Hord of Flies
Lies the compost loquaxt reveladed,
Flown carry-on new arkadine La Shellareine.

Lociss stations of the guillos vios way
Aweighted oraclay de-lighted,
Unguessed, unloved, the womb new Tao,
Trodden upon by automaton bronze was Talos
Turned the winged Talaris to Terra bi-lys est!

She was come forth discarded sorrow -
Io-clonnif curly temple. Oh everyone to know her!
Wood hare the cunnewayre! Be Dam A L'aundres with her!
Plunge pnew mania raling double terrasp lungs!

(Was somewhere hoped reduce her -
Baphomet Maide Moppet Pomme-Bomet,
A tidy piece of corruption hid from view three thousand years.
The gnostic glare, display of clarity undissembled,
Seemed near to cretin strange mask as wheezed above
The visage melted gelloid swollen mongoleonoid.)

Yet Maide even I, child of London town was Llew's,
To clutch receivership a doll...
Denigrate named her passivistic Dol Dol Orous!
Was easily torn or fallen apart!

Never as a child,
Did I look on newborn lain its cot or carriage,
Without cold flesh revulsion must turn away else swooned in faint....
Infants meant to me but unknown babes that lay there dead.
And dolls were things scarce different.
(Was to die my Io, child my own.
Littlest Lily, sundered Kuh-mingler Secundried with Death.)

Ah yes I thought...
Was all explained... dead babies and dead dolls,
Harbingering an aversion... a kind of foresight from long ago,
A warning.... Yes, and also no. There would come more.

Her limpid flesh so blue and cold. Oh, seen it all before...
One, and maybe two, had lain the metal slab beside me...
Were kindred mine? were dead?
(So paralyzed that lifetime terror,
Attendance on my own dead child
But multiplied its suffering thousandfold:
{ Tara doll apart! }
Rendered me not able to perform the solemn watch before
Her tiny corpse was lain there dead.)

Oh Mother. How many others known such?

To this day spring scars the tears
Are almost blood their tidings read:
Baby spirit hung and torn and quartered!

Crown of torns my skooll, my head.
Apaulus terrorbysmus set my shoulders
Is detruncate every night! tonight!
To grind it axe upon my soul,
Delve and slice the fathos
Divide from me detraxive wound its treasures,
Probe cells the tree a terabaumb
Maide violos to leave
Her every House, Hote haven...

No more Windsoared.
Replaced by current cousin.
From altitude shot down halfway Bu-canon was deployed
On Elizabeth the First's behalf.
Same Elizabeth did eternally assume its burden...
The tragic head decapitate belonged to Mary Stuart.

While is associate as well,
Elizabeth the mother to baptist Saint John,
Her son another martyr early lost his head,
As relic thence transported to its hallowed depths
The Green Hill lying far away
To gloom his night lain steraphim
Inside Gaull-Gotha's Gauld The Urn Field.

Seemed also fated green-hill death young Larry Hill,
Joyce's Hill-airy, James played Gimmy is James Joyce's other twin,
The Dummy UnMaidh or changeling,
And abducted by the prank queen Grace O'Malley,
Abhachdach Queen of Irish Joys.

Bereft one day, fear-fevered crisis,
Shown me was thing Maide of wax,
Dummy beheaded by Two-Swauds!

Ah. Near completed then! the terrar-smothered!

Yet now and even so, head once hung, held high Fé-Cundra understanding...
The Green Gau Cells foremessiters teach,

And Lune-Cow Kundimenta de Lalangt,
Joy Sillary Celirisibate New Hagnostic laughs risybil at lasst.
Wind soars Heil-Air, records hilarity redeeming:
Salutis, Lavia, Hilarrynx Lancoptric!

* * *

Maman:

Symbology finally vaulted... and overcome, the images your dreams....
Sister graduates of Her College L'Écologie The School Columbe;
Does Love attend and restore you,
WayFairers my daughters who circle cross your earth again.
As history convolutes, and as your souls foretell,
Once more are you brought together.
(***Do both of you know who I mean.***)

No more of death! Nor sentencing of prison time.
Apprenticed eighteen years
Again shall old love flourish:
Attain same tenacious strength
Coils hardy our vine blue grapple....

BOOK TWENTY-SEVEN

LES PROTOCOLS L'ÉCOLE COLOMBE

(Believed arrived the end of its existence, completed temporal life,

Essence as soul's vessel
Consoles itself jesucritical
By judging its mortality...
Requiring human world no longer,
Whatever the former semblance seen.)

Bah! I would end it! DEATH!
Hardly met the promise of politic new-formed: Religion of Redeemocrat!

What had it meant to you before this date...
Was rail... was Cundrie?
As infant, could you gesst,
Sickened close to death
Suffocate knewmania,
Exstase your breath is rale near ended?
Would d'ogham symbo-lie Apaulace stake,
Pague sufflebus palings ang-uish no return?

No! Maide incommunicado:
Helled Herren Guarden the babe preverbal,
Could but suffer it waifearos awaiting her commission,

For long was fallen paradise and eden.
After fallen, reads reversed ' nede dna-e-sidarap ':
Nidus the nest its siderus star, issued first compound stellar DNA.

The Lapsus Lapillus. Exilis: One of Slender Means, The Pauper-Stone.

Take new Techknowledge my Sonne-ology:
Etymolog-use! Little nediot!
Loo k'under! Nether. Look-under nidus is your nest
My nestling pytho, Oraculum Delphic Pytho-nesst!
(The oldest name for Del Phi, Oracle the Fish.
Its usage and entitlement assumed by royal line D'aufin:
D'oeuvres. W'oeuvres: Egg of lesser-known D'Oeuf-Fin.)

To you was represented that Dolphin met his end - the killing by Apollo!
Fin is end. But **end** *of Dolphin?*
Really? **The Fin?**
How shall this be? Dolph or Delph **(sans phin)** *means of the womb!*
And paradox further: Not! **Finn** *-ished first creatures The Maide's.*
Not Maide Complete. (Was mentioned before.)
So how may The End be entrapped in The Word?
Fostered on you falsely, Mere Mythtory!

Are none of you keyed in. Attained at best to humanist.
Isolate from The Word and World-stream, detached, you only observe:
Creatures servicing an organized bureaucracy unsuspected,
Set in place and milked by god of thieves and merchants
Employing representation is illusory,
Purveys its stuff as if was Maide complete Deannic,
By Isis-Minne-Venus-Aphro-Dite, Goddess spoke creation.

I AM THE MOTHER OF ALL THE LIVING. MOTHER TO THE DEAD.

A world was left in your keeping.
Came massacre therein and systematic killing:
Whole peoples slain by engineered contrivance was famine's deprivation;
Chronicled always by someone - somewhere -
Cadenced beautiful and measured - the requisite and lofty condemnation.

Jubbish!

Is nowhere addressed the whorling vortex that underlies the human heart-
A fundamental urge to genocide,
A-Polar force that seeks to draw all down;
Opposes any fountaining of virtue springing knowledgeable and innate,

Ever may genius write, glorify and paint, celebrate the debacle.
Yet where shall be found the genius-spirit to end it!

Maide this chalice my cup,
New Ark and everlasting covenant to you;
H'Arkening new herald, bore us bounteous in our hope
That now Blood was wedded The Highest on High,
The Nameless Immeasurable Below.

Carpe Diem Piscinensius! Yourself! must trust to Fish! for Truth!
Once You Found Me There!

So very late. Commune with me, my daughters
As to how may you tread new way.
Is bent forever, my first one.
Still! possible to do it better,
Lead you from the quagmire risen high about you...
Free you domination of the tribes came Male-Diction.

Fashion now the small and bowering groves...
Silent Sat your heart,
There shall you hear Me.

Availed you no such access,
Then make image of that heart,
Compare it with the flower.
Ponder the quickening petalling, beauty as your own -
Is but a day the planetary existence departed in its hour.

Yet! Crystalline are watered veins and cells reflective all the worlds.
Why Maide beauty fleeting except betokening bounty of the Mat-Eternal,
Your freely given earth?

Bring back that world!
Cherish. Else begone!

Gardened safety and soft dignity your place within it...
Advised again is study of that eden first provided,
Magic life was tampered with.
Sad distance are you strayed! your far arrival thus!

You would do well to contemplate conditions that shape your situation.
Make re-examination of these monographs are the briefs of Noter Damus:
Loosely strung their threading on a common theme of tragedy,
Tells them of the wrongs beset my children.

Murdered at the outset was pride of human soul and spirit.
The established ritual of antiquity... murder of body no longer is novel.

So no surprise your forfeit of autonomy and your natural right, respect.
Too certain the binding of Woman, crushed coilings agenda oppressive
Sees her but bartered flesh fit bridle-bound for market;
Is pythonic anaconda itself directed tutelage oracular,
Maide mouthpiece for Apollo, annunciate his dict-um....

(Was ever final neuro-circuitry connected its beginnings, never had
You needed die, nor be reborn therefore to flesh not self-renewing.)
Now life is borne new gestate - only certainty the flight sad-passaged
Speeds die-stressed before terrorist Death.

Ripartee denunciate at its funeral:
' Man that is born of Woman... ' Eh!
What then of man has borne his own seed?
And is therefore not! man who is born of Woman!

Naught but artifact rock-pelvic girdle cradled construct,
Newest infra-spawn In-Hu-Man, product of Apollo:
Who laboring sought only she be gone! Be damne! The Deltic Sin-Fold!)

Yet Men: Among you some the best were ever Maide...
Were detached amnesiac from the bonds your earth....
Were long ago seduced unknowing

Great phallusy you bare was instrument, attainment flown Her-Speritese:
Ensured Symballic Golden Fruit a limit on mortality.

Historic day how sad had made discovery,
Came also hence, paternity.

Let us weigh their aftermath, the politics engendered of such insight:

Perceived it very quickly Men, the masculine advantage,
And quick just so, to formulate the means whereby was subjugated Woman.
Estimate was, would take but little longer, then could she be removed.

(We refer to its early phase, the Apollyonic long plan:
Covert scheme expanded in our foreword.)

We can assess the progress.

Bred to custom so familiar,

Remaining unaware of bear-jerks on the chain,
You possess no freedom beyond constricted life within its measured reach.
Coercion to prod you passive:
Fine line defines acceptance as opposed to banishment and outlawry.
And as conformity appears to you protection,
Has undone you, herd-mentation.

Let us now field questions on the issue howsoever viewed is limited,
May even in an awful way not matter -
Is solely symptom of pathology looming infinitely greater -
Embroiling every woman unprepared in bitterness of fate amounts to ruin:
Generates the angst is so extreme,
Maide to founder agonized in empty prayer

' Should I kill myself?
Is suicide the only option?
Is my own life not my own?

Is it a sin to have an abortion?
Am I committing murder?
Is there a human being inside me from the start?
And if there is not, when does human life begin?

I do not wish to be pregnant.
I feel I should have an abortion
But am afraid of suffering for it in the future.
I have no money to pay for my own,
But I'm afraid of coat hangers, too.
How can I be absolutely sure
That this is right action for me and the baby?

I was raised in the Catholic Church and I am 15 years old. I am pregnant And my parents do not know. I do not want a baby, but I am scared of Going to hell if I have an abortion. I am terrified to tell my parents,

They'd never let me have one!
They tell me go to hell anyway.
What should I do? '

* * *

Child. Child. Can be no answer straight where all is bent. Plainly there is no solution more than partial. Compromise comes hard.

Not the soul is subject to biology arises space and time,

Those earthly realms wherein rotates the life is cellular,
Attains to Bardo ends... beginnings...
To births but presage the so-called death.

No. Not the soul to die:
The soul is state immortal where death is nonexistent,
Yet must navigate the nether slides of spirit when is abandoned flesh,
Fallen like the season's leaf departed sire eternal is its tree...
A viewing of life not yet begun,
Tree-world reminding of life without end.

Challenged by the hurdle, finite your flesh,
Uninstructed is organic by the soul.
Human! Now prepare to joust the polarized moralities are secular,
Palaver contumacious, their 'Abortion Issue!'

Hear argument the nightbrain: if foetus is to be,
Or not to be.
You are exhorted human life is sacred:
All and every part of it.
A consciousness may not be measured -
Lain sacrosanct its mystery.

Why you can't help but agree its an act of murder -
Destroying the helpless thing like that
Could never defend itself unless we do!
Even murder is not too big a price to pay
If that's what it takes to stop you. '
Then so saying, does.

Oxymoronic you shall hear,
How foetus is but parasite,
A cellular growth sustained in symbiosis with the mother,
While form not yet attained to viable life
Reproduces independently on a cellular level... able to maintain itself.
The process requiring but twenty-eight weeks.

We confront again that finite premise
Presuming life is inclusive of death...
Cells are either possessed of conscious soul,
Or proliferate as piece of lumpen flesh unquickened.

Oh neither! A soul is eternal. It may not die.
Therefore questions of its termination,
Or is converse addressed as some new and original birth,

Are verbal ploys to beg the issue,
To cloud (as ever) the verities of soul-life is eternal.

The soul may discard or assume any earth-skeined garment pleasing it.
Threads spelling qualities the DNA do not give a damn!

Soul itself must expedite! judge suitable the form next worn its karma.
Did you think was clay of flesh that chose the life-form it inhabits?

Do not misunderstand me. Truly, peril does crowd near.
And ravening jaws await each Woman's step Maide false,
To break her or replace her by any means are foul.

If believed, the current propaganda...
Either way gone pro or con,
Then are you duped.
Should clarity stare beyond all dialectic,
Then are you labelled and pursued, ' freethinker '.

It can not matter what you think.
Your belief or disbelief.
Your head is embattled false logic.
Trod even once beyond its boundaries you are human marked:

‘ Woman Who is Fallen ’...
Or perhaps protected camouflage unnoticed,
*Bred The Bridled Mechanical Bride. **

Deep my condolence. My blessing.

*   *   *

*The Mechanical Bride, Marshall McLuhan.

BOOK TWENTY-EIGHT

A WORLD RENEWED

I Am The Mother Of All The Living, Mother To The Dead.

Forever Proscribed: On, Or To This Planet, The Dealing Of Death.

Be aware are yours and also mine,
Those spirals DNA, Maide cementics set reality,
Are Sat-Creatures every one comprising Our Body....
And therefore shall never be eaten any sort of kine:
For all flesh formed is Flesh of Our Own.

I would have no predators, nor beasts of prey.

The lust to kill is the lust for death:
Temptation an ultimate wish for oneself to die,
And sin to me accounted crime;
Exposed you mortal to the logos faulty root satanic served base premise,
Would enslave or else remove you,
He who yet remained the unknown other.

Relapses violent the carnivore, is bloody and offensive,
Recidivistic as succumbs to canapolos anger,
Long patterned to repeat.
Tutored proclivity such, follows hard the sickness subsequent
On lust indulged continuous, its addiction abbatoirical.

You who had partaken of life-forms eaten...
Were not informed that all did stem same tree was branched your own!
An appetite begotten Death for you!

I have provided foods are more benevolent and enhancing.
Does suffice old knowledge explores its Khymisteries The Orgonomic,
Re-animates the linkaged systems are microscopic worlds,
That fused, were shared new-bred
With Master Cells Le Vi Athonice.

Yet long ago, lost Eden.
Entered pustulant apustle, thing creepeth Abo-Minne -
And introduced De-vile A-Sat:
Then came Aphollowmen his throughout all time.

S'Appel Cain et Abel are known as abberrants insane -
Fratridic caniborts compounding tragedy,
But never universally apprised the truth of murderous stratagem
Earned you guerre-donor reward....
Howsobeit, imperative is your retrieval of the memory:
How first was eaten The Apolophagus!
Cur-tailed Genetrix Aphollowed ever after.

Anathema! The cannibal.
Proscribed, the brutishness unnatural partakes of creature flesh.

RESOLVE ON THE KILLING OF DEATH!

Outlaw assuredly, Money:
The banker's stall, his taberna argentarius.
Neutralize oppression A-Policy backed by gold,
Its various ploys of usury and fiduciaries
Implicit used against you.

(You alone are The Gold Fleeced!
Needed no slaughter the ram!)

Barter instead the fruits of your earth: handiwork, talents your own.
In setting those boundaries personal -
There is holding of limit on hoarding.
Tally your wage by your output -
Reflecting the sum of your social exchange.

Be wary too of merchandise boasts of value only calculate the market:
Are gifts of nature less complex and use your own labor... almost free.

Should no one be impelled that service
Outstripped them of talent or scope,
Yet can all be found the appropriate task
Fits each woman's skill and constitution.

Establish food banks. Yes.
Distribute each day as accorded its need:
Examined then certified wholesome. Nontoxic.
Proper contained, not to perish.

Serious contention arousing the blood...

Shall hostility be subdued those certain ways remaining fair;
Devise them otherwise than mortal kill....
And persist no more in chronic feud tormented you...
Declare instead for tournament is formal....

Grievance resolve by conduction of sport nonblooded,
Contest of battle hymn challenged with music
Overcomes by soaring sounds of exaltation over what was base.
And, honorable reinstate them,
Those trials of strength determined hand to hand

Established body-mind endurance....
Restore them, Goddess' Nature Games honored long ago:
The Games of prowess. Games of skill.

Dedicate to me, your theatres.

Now subverted tinny instrument and mouthing exi-stenchal,
Drama once was vital art provided total teaching and immersion,
Addressed the fledgling soul as rapt absorbed its message.

Meticulous drawn were battle lines,
The kinds to teach moralities engendered no reprisal!

Women! More devoutly must you seek out education.
Not that pursuit of so-called equality with the male,
But to exercise potential already is possessed,

Whether this be conscious soul magnetized the arts,
Or management - or child care -
Studies farmagique or manual tends the herbivore,
Engages itself in any manner of career.
Now do we ask of you, skilled creator-crafters all,

That you provide and cherish familial homes ensured the nurture everyone.

And if not quite created that fabled Summer Land Aeterna,
Be sure, that bonded covenants these
Set the social limits more equal,
And better world you still might have...
Providing any one fulfillment... enjoyment of satisfactions peaceable.

If should seem at first new mainstream life
Condition less than prodigal,
Dazzling not so pyrotechnic as befitted ersatz erstwhile was assumed...
Would be found soule-energies enhanced to balance it,
Deliver you from the frenzy unconsolable,
Comes consequent on consuming, leaching,
Chronic leaves you suffering lack that can not be defined.

But liberated are you meanwhile
From abject your former status:

The minion lowly, age-old prey served golden fleecing...
Sacrow-sunk Apollo roamed companionate hungry predator pack...
Human his wolf.

And counteracted Fear of Death, ought Ceres-Monics be revived again,

To teach once more of Eleusinging Joy of Life
That savors love enacted breath of flowering earth
Rose hence immortals' heaven....

Yourselves must inculcate these precepts:
Let love be focused on each other;
Let there be trust for the one who has Maide you.
Organic key comes every life, sustains itself as gives itself,
Nourishes its world's soul - joined all others.
Pleine soul is our soul. Plain heart is our heart.

Despite all burdening ignorance inherited tragic as your portion,
Know thankfulness for pardon
That you may not really sin within the dream was but a state unknowing -
Nor really harm the world soul, while in your souls you could not know.
Ignorant and unfinished, you neither truly warrant blame nor punishment,
But there exists due process teaches for oneself what justice means
(So long as is granted same pardon to others):

' You have no defenses. Nor may you judge.
Until you know, you must believe. '

*   *   *

Oh curbs them well, the scourge Apollo!
Subservience is ensured him...

Faim frail et mal-hemale, newly created he them,
To live the evil lived anti-life.
Initiate brute or hammered him timid, bondsmen implacable, all:
Incendiary demons, conditioned in torment,
In anguish ongoing of pseudograph burning....
But lately devised that conception... mortal deceit is his Hell.

Or converse, belief denied in afterlife,
Are those to exist ' in the here and the now '...
Of harrowing hell or delight come from heaven, to dwell in isolation...
Blanketed and insulate against supposed immunity to guilt,
Think evil but a thing contrived, political threat offering anti-life.

I note this random night of Janus, Annus MCMXC
(Years not dated nephilim, nor recorded Duvel Io: Anno-Dominatrix),
The world is on the very eve of war.
Hear it! EVE! Name-snaked only after her! the wars mankind's.

(Quit the Garden good and aye,
Why not poised on very ***Adam,*** *war?*
Too close suggested Adam tomb was Atom?
Too close suggested Damned, A Dame?
Was A-dam then A-woman?)

Sacred womb, a tomb housed constant conscript!
Be Daemned! Are massacred our children!
Reduced the blood-slake, Moloch wars!
Hear oh Daughters!
Send no more your boy-child as army's sacrifice inducted!

Bitter howsoever be the end
You must yet protect him staunch.
Refuse it, scythe gleaned sacrilijahs,
Tythe exacted wanton, blood child sweet your own.
Consigned him macerate was nameless,
Rendered him anonymous,
Left godless faceless stuff coerced Death's breach!

Now lies peace alone the sheltered garde!
Has freedom longtime not existed,

But for narrow coffin, limit was defined.
Containment manifest and understood!
The common use of legal boundary.

* * *

From nurture of the very soil subverted:
Constructed eager is New Adom-Atom-breeder our reactor.

Student turned perversity,
Plans and fans the nationalistic fervor,
Irrational radish turncoat
Nurtures racist-radic-international.

But riveted kept isolate, captured by hypnosis;
Vox controls him, silphorescent boundary framed unmoving,
As selects the adam TV Deo voudovile diversion,

Zombie rendered subject to the feudal lord another sort:
Harvests him and raises him hybred couch potato,
While despising, dismantling, the scaffold his mind -
T.V. Voler, Medea oracular; thief fleeced all the world.

Tenant differs little from the middle ages,
Except imprisoned his own private castle... set apart his cubic cell,
Captive of de-mediocrity futile held the feudal manor,

Harried screen of plated silver, spooned swallow-stone TV
De-mock crazed the persuasion seeming gentle:
' Product ours, you must buy, buy. And enemy ours, you must kill. '

Effusion no discussion otherwise.

We do not know how you will fare should new war be declared.
Always is it there!
Is railed within your Kundread hearts.

(Inspired the Dogma-Amen,
Sing over bagwhag Ah Men Ra this very night,
The worship Gog-Lord-Magog!)

For such beseechings babbylon,
Should Woman smite them harrowing.
She does. She did.
(Had she but Bhagd Dad's sperm instead...
Then saved was soldier dead and body-bagged.)

Once borne muscled mosque-limb, crescent was Her aegis.
Shuffle now the streets their women burka swathed,
Faces hid and shielded yashmak
Was supposed deflection, shunt naive,
Of Great Satan's evil eye... of intrusion staring rapine.

Shame! The yoke of men alone to place them there!..
Cunic punic warrn the mask of muffled chattel....
Yet tending homes against their return, those manly rebels
Hobbled rabble swarmed the country,
Defying, threatening, screaming war. Rabbilis est.
That! is their activity.
That! the rabid mob to terrorize the world unmuzzled.

Incapable of work or peace does each pretender strut,
Zealot proposed strange peace portrayed in his own image;
Rallies assemblies tell a vision war machines,
Unleashes terrorists are brainwashed,
Weak circuitries implanted with the plunderous lust to kill.

Can wait forever Coo Wait it seems. And Dove Be Damned!
As swallows coup small country whole, Sadam Insane his slipper-y sins!

World self-unsustaining,
Undergoes destruction wholesale,
Degraded lies about you, blood-flay stripped its skin,
Pressing out the mighty pulsing fuel its heart's blood
Pumped Black-Gold, New World Sovereign, Oil.

Resource exceeding this and even less renewable, provender is vanishing:
All new growth of forest Tree-collective, your Braintree Cell is life!

Genesis occurring before was reveladon, was treachistory The Fall.
Become the creatures co-arse were once my mayking,
Ruled by money mono-keyed Ap Hanuman D'or, the monarkeyng coeurupting,
Agitprop piping a world to its folly.

(Begat thereat, fell Ladan to Apollo.
Heady fruit the pommes d'amour did mouthon fellatio eat.
No Sun God is Apollo, he is but God of Death.
Yes. I-accus... my dear!)

First was Mini-Replicu *led*
That world accorded other order,
My own and former giant planet.

Next were sundry artifacts devised,
Tooled fresh minted for boundless service,
Set up conformation, our own familial templates:

Treasure new, Anatomy Yours:
The value transcending all other.

Wrapt the body such as that,
Needed what from the world beyond pleasure?
Keyed to containment within it,
What else desired spirit to conjure,
Laved by enveloping sheath of miraculous kined,
Skeine Maide Mannas' Laver Hlafdige,
Not alone by bread of earth sustained?

Maide from the stars:
Intended to shine internal their light,
But light beclouded, neither served nor illumined the way.
There had been a world came love and tenderness -
Safe the lambs to frolic innocent about their shepherdess -
World to flourish, had they won no place, the militant expansionists,
Minions hostile. Sparrows of the minor gods.

(Nor yet required for planet's life continuation,
That final interval become necessity:
Sometimes kindly! Death...

Pause octavate strums propagate ongoing life,
Long-Body culminating time sol-astral to then recur new birth New Human,
Goes clad again fresh life form, creates ongoing variation.)

But lost their balance, the mechanics stabilizing earth,
Are systems losing virtue... running down.

Maide the self-sustaining, now is skewed its orbit;
Internal flux and wobble buckles globe of earth,
And plates the deepest bindings are dismantled inexorable
By maimed, corrupted asses, by those donkeys Set in place.

Apollicy meant to sink it.
Rock fabric space, celestial body, rotted rodent spore...
Plagued incursion too prolife-rat. Diaspo-rat.
No. He does not Apolloguise.

This! The original sin - by which the world was won.

Its sweetness destroyed... its soundness.
A planet stocked through aeons created garden paradaiza.
Loveliness was legend... primal forest, tallest trees....
Grain and seed so plentiful,
Subsisted creature every sort....
Ages spent... the making....

Then quick was nurturing garden stripped;
Whipped ferus spearhead spirit of the air,
Worldwind lethal, torched its oil;
Scorched hell's breath devastation the Apolluted fume
Wrote signature of cartel Hu Manic Wars.

Happened even did Apallow slide those many moons above sulphuric clouds
Plumed darkest night ungently drew
Each set of ralè'd lungs pneumoaned
That groaned instead of wept,
Struggled vaporous breath beseeched polluted heaven:

' *Lady Lave au Laundres! Reign!*
Rain particulate as you will! But Rain!
Hasten and preserve us from Poll-Uttoman sent hell!

Scour and lave Your Heavens! Make them breathable again!
Or suffocate stopped us, birking fume ubiquitous,
Writhed towering smudge sul-fury substitute the air. '

*   *   *

Think on it!
In the beginning
Had not occurred such thing as mortal Death.

Walked hand in hand our progeny the sweetest aisles of perfect earth...
Risen there its soil, spread holy stock organic membrane woven round...

And close to his completion, Ladan:
Near finalized were suprafaculties to promise fullest life.

Although comprised of virtue seemed dependable -
Passing few the centuries that saw the root corrupted,
And virtue breeched did not appear again.

(Yet was accorded but single afternoon,
In the time-scale spent my own.)

And do you retain no memory that reinstates the earthly dream maide Gau?
Of A-Pollot punishing Ladan poulish? No. It is apparent. You do not.

Long ago, in contemplation of his image did Apollo split himself as two.
Born heaven twinned were polarized the halves his selves and pauperized.
Isolant and desolant... such majesty remaining was cast in its own pit...
Languishing detention of the clamored frolic flesh.

(But gods are principles fixed. And may not change.
If resolved on obtaining a soul, they must undertake life as a human.
Then is the fundament divine relinquished as new mortal enters Bio-Time.

And should it deteriorate, that human soul,
Become confined as crystal is circumscribed its limit,
Then whosoever undertakes his soul's reassembling
Is compelled in addition to endure its heart's breaking.)

Paints him Tintoretto,
Attempting reconcile a polar gnostic north as hermaphroditic Mundus Rex:
Poled Bi-Acchus frozen Dianiesus, portraying impotence and rage
Defining fracture is his world -
Mirrors lusts of bacchsyphic greed, accompanied appetites castrati....

Blighted the earliest compassion; bore messianic its latter-day rot,
The head adjudicate alone, shown motivated malice, eroded virulence.
Oh had never twain been Man invented!

Broken polar by Apollo. Then divided formed him second.
So why was egg and dart thus parted?

Daughter. Not so hard a riddle!
Accorded misfortune original plan

' Shall be thy desire to thy husband...
Shall he rule over thee .... '

Pressed Flesh Crown Orpithorn Maide subject human rule and reproduction
Lusted after power of gold and offered sister's world, destruction.

And did mousey misfits fissured...
His servants smintheus, mine it.

Yet is nowhere introduced full theme:
Of significance more than Hate of Twin,
Exists the Hate of Woman!

(While converse, can sentiments stated be proved untrue:
Empty mask that so-called ' Love of Man ' lying genuine in nothing!)

Exists hermaphrodite entanglement in dual skein...
To caper Woerhm and Aphrodite.
To ever yearn that former blessed, wholeness;
Reappointment to that severed dual matrix.
Concept overlooked is love...
And no solution this, providing perfect;
Only guaranteed perpetual the motives grim ungratified.

Isolate in twin-dependence,
Yet thwarted each! to lack the other...
Orpanquinity between them the state they really sought,
Clung deluded to obstructions were themselves,
Contriving juxtaposition more than any could be natural,
To deny not reconcile the aeon-life aversion...
Attempt surpassing so-phistronic! Impossible be borne!

My Human Maide the first,
Never known frisson was lightning charge antipathy,
Malignancy afflicted first the gods.

* * *

Devised his curse, Apollo,
Set Man against The Woman. The descendants human & kine.
Yet had not early surged such enmity between the genders,
Persecuted first, The Queen of Heaven.
Aphollowed only after...
Churst and Massacred, The Woman.

Offal equal entertainment malpano-prop-aggranda to the goose
That **lays** *the golden eggs,*
And offered no pretense of serving goddess other than herself,
Is Woman overwhelmed by apollunic forces
Easily turning her to their will.

He bruises heel, Apollo:

' Upon your seed, my venmity.
Serpent Worman! Repent! '
Harries her, Impalla-Acchus,
Self-proclaimed was Jealous God
Impelled the rancor ancient.
As perceives the beauty envied Maide New Human,
Twinned progeny was Io's,

Sets about its persecution
Causing you henceforward
Vengeful mayhem and destruction.
Trampling you as herded chattel
Derogates as produce hardly more than beasts the fields,

Reached to genocide, the earthly state of war between your human sexes.
Yet never existed true schism, except was thing contrived in heaven.
So not come first the struggle separates the sexes.
Yet conditioned equal are Male and Female,
Denying both, their maker goddess.

The Woman now transferred by husband's contract,
Maide ' property ' the legal bridled chattel,
Woeuvered wifely rights to body-celebrant
Is veiled and ' given ' thus in marriage.

(Goes also veiled the fact that Wife-new-Maide is delivered to possession,
And shrouded equal
The etymology of Brid-ale-veiled and Bride-well,
The two of them houses intent on correction -
Where womens' tears spring prison cell.)

Oh. Until the Exultation
Day Couvade The Vater Father

(In-Vader Man-New-Woman Hatcheteth,
And you set six feet under)...

Pending coup accomplished makes Coo-Vades the fathers,
Are complicitous truths accepted still
As honor old testorment patri-arch-official dictum:

Soule-privilege hers, existence uternational,
To last as long... the auto-uteronomy bred children.

(Upheld at least the durance -
Bright New Dawn assuring Uter-Neuter -
When shall be The Living Womb of Spouse
Exchanged conspiracy ' In Vitro ' by innocence of glass.)

Admired perpetual, accepted and approved by peers,
They do yet receive their compliments full measure,
Messeoir D' Hernetree, The Breeding Groom
And blushing brede his dam...

Yet arriving even now the menace patriar-culled,
Land Poppycock the New Cockayne!

Before deluged the waters drowning doodledoo!
Was every egg made perfect in blessed ignorance of the cock-a-spurmed...
Cock'né egg lowborn in truth!
Born un-bridled prospect, produce archi-ficial,
Now delivers cock-né A-poulet his first afreet!

Mounts Apoulet His Template night-mère spawn on monstrous womb
Jabs reel of spinning life is modified new reprogene -
Fathering democrazy was designed immaculate to replace you,
An unholy host conception of the artifact emasculine
Helled you plastic metalled birth-machine:
Ghouly host The Tubal Billy.
Let him!

Via courier vialled frozen sperm, provenance The Late and Former Earth,
Yourselves prepare for soul-survival in another place.
Accorded with Corea, resume the attribution Woman, Natural Sovereign,
Gone somewhere else impregnate (prerogative assuredly The Female's)...
Could Exodus happen again!

BOOK TWENTY-NINE

A POLICY AGAINST APOLLO

The politics? Pah! Stop breeding.
Imposed no tool of vengeance, chastity;
Yet wielded power of bargaining
Restored world rule to women.

Au contraire: My Ordinance accepted,
Then Women!
Negotiate conveyance reinstated Woman once again Supreme,
Assumed control of food, condition as before:
Entailed, Maide legal, Descendancies Female Your Lands.

Cease and Desist: All Reproductive Traffic.

Where equality exists can be no enslavement.
Shall no patriarchal will control the reproductive process,
Replicated Woman human, or humble female beast.
Shall no organic womb of any species be exploited.

Freak-went high places, Napoleonic Nicolas, Le Msr. Chauvin:
Long amongst you his devotees, rapists vicious, who violate contemptuous
Their random victims -
Crime held neither sufficiently abhorrent nor properly chastised, but is

Sly condoned by civic fathers patriarchal
Are themselves implacable spearheads of direct and covert aggression.

What consequence the infant is born of rape one more?

Yet until is structured the scaffold secure supporting Woman's evolution,
And you believe you are fertile...
A policy conceivable is that you hide.
Has not yet dawned the day sees rapist sterilized.

Against the perpetration of mindless impregnation,
Arrange programs provided for austerity.

Ensured sterilization of human sperm, needs no woman undergo abortion -
Remember, declining of espousal does not equate with male to be removed.

Neither punished nor destroyed bright masculine wick
Snuffs women lepidopteral in its flame....
Yet imperative is your vigilant resistance.
And if not to extent reached blood-let,
Or howsoever is desired nonmilitant,
Certain a war of some kind is declared.

Computed living data comprising systems psycho-biophysical,
Relayed in perpetuity by the planet-consciousness inherent,
Displays perfections its assessment in beauties arabesque -
Now advising welfare programs of its own.

Needs be reduced the burgeoning community is formed organic life upon it.
Failing this, accomplished is the world decline of creature spermatazoa.
To date, reduced by Silent Sperm is the DNA that links and escalates
The Life Tree from molecule to Manicule.

By-product ignoranus is the current plague of phagotry -
Concomitent with its unexpected ailment - AIDS -
A failure of immunities within systems breached swift by random attack,
Its victims' days are counted finite, ending sundry spin-off variation.

To these afflictions, add new dominance of virus life...
Whereby organic integrity is disturbed,
Microworlds that coexisted fairly peaceful on the planet,
Rampage virulent new outbreak as carriers viral of the air.
And by any count of time on earth,
Three single days will see their transport global,
Hosted by the common carrier is your aircraft.

* * *

Your sons top-gallant to oeuvre-master you,
Privileged, they are haughty,
Lack the heart that considers... is well bred.
And A-Polled new the phallic mast,
Lead lives but pecca-dildo:
Bacchtermystic interlewd to death.

Women!
By their god they are bred to hate you!
Has Dyontissues cost The Goddess Mat
Dominion lost - Maide the Planet.

* * *

Lofted serpent trail My Cradle Ship of needling spire and pinnacle,
Capable of all things, the descending spearing light,
When was focussed solar fire for earth.

Dove your space to part the waters,
Dwelled island homes were sunk deep fathoms lain beneath their lakes.

I, whose vessel skimming undulate seemed as serpent curling heaven...
Was in truth your goddess come again to nurture.

Ship mine, the primal image not forgotten:
Is replicated every churchly steeple graced its hamlet...
Wherein preacher now ensconced intones abbe-rant ex cathedra
The age old hollowness of words so-fisticulate Aphollow's:

' Understand the thrust of form is but a thing symbolic:
A-Spiring worship promised Adam resurrection from his death. '
Perhaps to thence deliver him, blown to bits by missile shaped a-spire.

Yet covenant once was Maide and given:
Never Should You Die!
Maide and taught you from our Eden,
That Eden was Our Earth and Soul.

Hlafa Maide the Loaves of Breed,
Maide them Little, the Fishes:
Holy Mass Hlafmaestress then their Soul divided,
Hlafweard risen Manna's Spirit
Flesh could not divide, or be divided.

Yet occurs not always tiding gentle, enunciate the angels....
I have loosed directive, thing is nearest answer,
Banished death....

Woman! Close the breech!
Present no more your sacred Self.
Neither lend nor lease your womb again.
All semen gird about!
(Simple is her symbol, Womankind:
Turtle lying supine, helpless on her back.)

But she fights for Death to end
As executes and lives my Words and Counsel!
Ceases now the palsied swarm proceeded pulsing spew
Of accursed amd hopeless loins.
Does sperm and rut refuse,
Does sterilize and chasti-gate:
Does utilize the means are any....

Possessing her Self,
The Fountained Life,
Champions it guarded as holy the fortress!

And on every form insemination,
Be it natural or was ' arranged ' ,
Terminates all gateway further,
Denies her doors, bail-weighted cargo,

On berth is Apalloined
On Seed is Appol-Man's Get.

Listen Well, My Daughters!

Secure and Seal All Entrance
Opened Wombs on Life!

Forerunners of New Guardians:

ELECT NO MORE TO BREED!